LEGENDS
OF STEAM

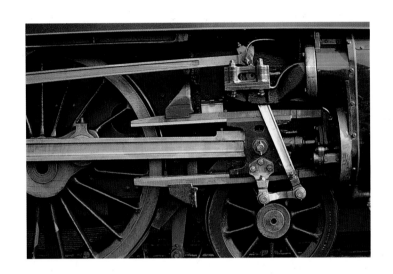

LEGENDS
OF
STEAM

COLIN GARRATT

SEVEN
DIALS

CONTENTS

INTRODUCTION

HALF A MEADOW away from the studios of Milepost 92½, nestling in the trees, is the Victorian bridge from which I watched my first trains over half a century ago. Steam trains were going to last forever; the first diesels and electrics simply added variety – an innocent belief in a blissful childhood through which locomotives of every shape, size, family and vintage roared, wheezed and shrieked.

Then, one morning in 1955, the magic was shattered when my father showed me the headlines of the *Daily Telegraph* announcing the British Railways Modernization Plan under which steam was to be phased out. But steam was at the heart of Britain's transport; experts stated that it could not possibly disappear before the end of the century. But they were wrong; the decimation of Britain's 20,000-strong steam fleet was destined to occur within just thirteen years. The magic was shattered and the most animated of man's creations – which cast a spell for a million happy childhoods – disappeared from our midst.

With the dying steam locomotive came the rise of motorways and the move towards a road-based economy. Line closures began which culminated in the devastation of the Beeching years in the mid-1960s, when upwards of 50 per cent of Britain's railway network was closed in an act of irreparable social mischief.

The precedent for all this had been set in America, where airlines, cars and heavy trucking had greatly reduced the nation's dependence on railways. There, part of the railways' attempts to compete and retain whatever traffic it could, was to dieselize, and long before British Railways' Modernization Programme was conceived, the American steam locomotive had been largely consigned to history. It was evident that following the lead of the West, country after country would ultimately declare against steam, and when the last British locomotive ran in August 1968 it was obvious that a world-wide revolution was under way, not just in motive power but also in modes of transport as well.

It was then that I made the decision to abandon a career in marketing to document the last steam locomotives of the world. Someone had to do it. The steam locomotive had been the heart-beat of the Industrial Revolution and Britain's greatest technological gift to mankind. From its very beginnings it provided a source of endless fascination; it was such an animated and flamboyant a part of our heritage that it could not and should not be allowed to vanish into oblivion without someone making a visual record of how the epoch came to an end.

Today, thirty years later, some fifty countries have been covered in three decades, during which my work has always been a desperate race against time. In producing this book, my brief from the publisher was to make it the finest visual tribute to the steam train ever published, and I am proud to include a few pictures from Ron Ziel of New York and A.E. 'Dusty' Durrant of South Africa, both world names as experts on the legend of steam. I am also fortunate to have combined with railway artist Terry Hadler, whose work appears interwoven with the photographs.

The standard gauge railways of Turkey (TCDD) had to overcome many operating difficulties, and it is hardly surprising that well-tried and tested German technology was chosen, well-suited to rigorous operating conditions. Here a standard two-cylinder 2-10-0 No 56.140 is seen on the Erzurum–Erzincan line in eastern Turkey.

Terry, like many of us, was brought up on railways in the heyday of steam; looking back, he recalls that the sun always shone; the summers were endless and laced with the smell of creosote from wooden sleepers, hot oil, sulphur and steam from the locomotives. He subsequently attended art college, and today is noted for military, naval, aviation and railway paintings. The paintings in this volume are taken from a selection of 100 specially commissioned by the publisher Ted Smart and took 2¹⁄₂ years to complete.

Terry lives in Oxfordshire in the heart of England, and parallel to his commissioned painting, he lectures in art and design. He attributes most of his success to his partner Margaret, who has done much to inspire and encourage him to put on to canvas his vivid memories of those 'golden days'.

Interestingly, my discipline as a photographer stems from the study of paintings. Of course, I have been aware of railway photography and am familiar with the works of the masters over the last 150 years, but my main inspiration was from the great painters to whom I turned in search of a pictorial language. To me, the greatest railway picture of all time is not a photograph, but a painting – Turner's *Rain, Steam and Speed*, of 1844, which celebrates the linking of London and Exeter by Brunel's magnificent 7ft gauge main line. The train is portrayed dashing across Maidenhead Viaduct during a squally storm in the Thames Valley.

And what of the hare racing for its life ahead of the train – Turner's way of relating the speed of nature with that of the machine, man having never travelled so fast. But we now live in an age of digital photography; such elements can now be added to our pictures. Magpies can be added to line-side fences to resemble the one which appeared in Monet's classic snowscape *The Magpie*. But perhaps I should say now that no picture in this volume has been digitally enhanced, all are as taken from nature.

Rain, Steam and Speed sits in London's National Gallery close to Turner's immortal *Fighting Temeraire*, depicting one of Nelson's fleet from Trafalgar being towed by a brand-new tug, which jubilantly belches a pall of smoke into the sunset. The *Temeraire* is being towed to its last mooring place, at which this British institution is to be broken-up. The tug in all its virility represents the new Age of Steam and contrasts with the *Temeraire*, depicted as a pallid phantom, a ghost from a bygone age.

Turner makes a distinction between the Age of Steam and Sail, and the two eras they represent. The caption which Turner appended to the painting reads: 'the flag which once braved the battle and the breeze no longer owns her'. Turner's incomparable canvas is, I believe, a far better memorial than had we physically preserved the Temeraire in dry dock.

During my early years of world expeditions I used to go to the National Gallery to see these pictures and would gaze endlessly at their magic; not just the brilliant execution of composition and colour, but also to reflect on their rhetorical aspects; the history and the society they represented. A picture may be worth a thousand words, but to me, the best pictures are those about which a thousand words need to be written.

The task of locating the world's surviving locomotives has always involved long research, as does the planning of complicated world expeditions and rasing the money to finance them, but these pall to insignificance when compared with the photographic challenge. Railway photography is not easy; the weather obviously plays a dominant role, especially with moving trains, when the sun must be out at the split second the subject passes. This presents little problem in sunny regions of the world, but in many areas, not least Europe, it is easy to spend

A Chinese industrial class SY Mikado 2-8-2 at Shenyang locomotive sheds; it is waiting to enter Shenyang works.

Valve gear details, draw hooks, emblems, numberplates and injector exhaust pipes from around the world.

days just to get one picture. For all the brilliance of today's cameras and the breathtaking quality of colour films, combined with digital creativity, there is still no substitute for sunlight.

Finding the right location is also manifestly difficult; distracting and irrelevant elements that spoil a picture's cohesion and expressiveness are everywhere, obvious examples being poles and wires, but there are a million more. In these respects the painter's task is easy; he or she can command the quality of light, decide what will be left in or out, change perspective at will, and above all else, can alter the density in which competing elements are painted. Photographic film recognizes no such nuances, and records competing elements every bit as strongly as the subject itself.

Quite apart from its animation, the steam locomotive is a sensuously beautiful creation. So which of the pictures in this book come closest to capturing the magic? An obvious example are the sunlight, smoke and shadow themes of pages 108–11. These epitomize the smoky intrigue of the steam sheds. In contrast, the study on page 92 of a fleeting train captures movement by way of composition and smoke trail; it shows the 'full train', which was one of the golden rules of the early railway photographers. And it is headed by a Pacific, the symbol of speed. One may recall in *Rain, Steam and Speed* how the train 'literally dashed across the canvas'. The superb sweep of perspective as the coaches recede into the distance

Axlebox and spring details from the tender of a former LMS Stanier 8F 2-8-0.

and the three swirls of steam issuing from the chimney, which serve to propel the train forward at an alarming pace – Thackeray estimated a speed of 50mph (80km/h)!

Terry's painting on page 252 of the American Mogul coming into a busy switching yard evokes the magic of the railway at night. One imagines it to be a warm summer evening with the sounds of shunting engines and clanking wagons filling the air in those years when the beat of the railway was the pulse of the nation.

I also love Terry's picture of the London & North Western Precursor 4-4-0 on page 87. There was something mystical about the LNW express passenger classes. See the wonderful apparition of the rebuilt Claughton on page 33. The fact that no LNW twentieth-century passenger locomotive has been preserved obviously heightens their allure. To my lifelong regret, I never saw any of them; they bore mystical names in their hundreds – quite the best ever chosen for any group of locomotives: *Sirocco, Ionic, Velocipede, Landrail* and *Suvla Bay*. LNW express passenger engines haunt my mind like a bevy of pre-Raphaelite women; to me, Crewe is not a town, it is a beautiful feeling.

If I be allowed one last indulgence, the Indian X series represent classic British 1920s steam, which was every bit as stylish as the music of that 'roaring decade'. Look at the XE on page 115, while its high-stepping express passenger relation, the XC on page 117, exudes the nostalgic atmosphere of the last survivor of a great breed, eking out its final days on menial tasks – in this case, the Bolpur pick-up freight. All the last XCs were allocated to Burdwan and dismally relegated to heavy shunting.

However, I hope that this book is seen to be free from the prejudices that have always bedevilled the study of railways. Evolution is not confined to rigid types in specific places; there is, for example, an exciting relationship between a Gresley P1 and an Indian Railway's XE. The LNER enthusiast might claim that he is not interested in India's locomotives, but, as the years pass, these prejudices will break down and the Steam Age will be seen as an exciting range of interrelated influences and schools of thought. It is wonderful to present railway lectures to schools and find an interest in steam that is devoid of preconceived ideas; this book is for such people.

A study of railways, like the study of natural history, is without limitation. So monumental was the Railway Age that anywhere that was anywhere had trains of some sort or another – and usually a variety. Today, the thousands of different types that have roamed the earth over the last two centuries are reduced to a relative handful, although, incredibly, brand-new engines emerging from China's Tangshan Works contrast with 125-year old Victorian survivors in neighbouring India.

The Steam Age, and the Industrial Revolution it drove, has been one of the most colourful periods in human history; perhaps the most colourful, and it is fitting that it be celebrated in a work like this. For when the last fire is finally dropped, only pictures such as these will remain to tell future generations of one of the greatest legends of all time. Consider the picture on page 102. Perhaps one Christmas morning in the year 2060, a child will open a present; it will be a jigsaw, and on the cover will be that picture with the caption 'Historic Steam Train on Sugar Plantation' and the child will wonder at the amazing apparitions that were once the wheels of industry. Will he know that this humble tank engine was the last of thousands that left Britain's shores to drive the Industrial Revolution around the world? One morning in the year 2060.

Colin Garratt
Milepost 92 ¹/₂
Newton Harcourt
Leicestershire

The setting sun throws into sharp focus the superb design of the Russian P36 4-8-4, which was one of the most exciting latter-day steam designs built in the face of impending dieselization.

CENTENARIANS *The world's oldest steam locomotives*

IN common with humankind, very few locomotives have ever become centenarians. During the formative years of steam development, change was rapid and the average life of locomotives during the first half century of their existence was on average fifteen years. But, as the railway expanded and locomotive types settled down into basic forms, niches appeared for engines to be downgraded or, in a few cases, simply to remain in their original capacity.

The world's centenarians date from the 1870s onwards. The most dramatic examples left in world service date from 1873 in the form of two metre (3ft 3⅜in) gauge 0-4-0 tender engines named *Tweed* and *Mersey*, which survive in sugar mill service in India. Both were built at Sharp Stewart's Great Bridgewater Street works in Manchester, and when the veterans left Liverpool Docks for India, Queen Victoria had another 28 years to rule the British Empire. These two engines are almost certainly the oldest extant today.

India takes third place with another metre gauge veteran. This one, an E class mixed traffic 0-4-2 tender engine, also in sugar mill service, was built by Dübs of Glasgow in 1876, as one of an early standard type for the emergent metre gauge railways of the subcontinent.

The only other known location for active centenarians is Cuba where a number of Baldwin-built tank engines survive, again in sugar mill service. The oldest of these is an 0-4-2 saddle tank, with 1882 emblazoned on her builder's plate.

Very few passenger engines survived to such ages, but a wonderful exception was the Indonesian B50 class 2-4-0s – another product from Sharp Stewart's legendary works. The 2-4-0 was one of the earliest forms of passenger locomotive. The type evolved during the 1830s and the Javan survivors represented a living link with the very origins of locomotive development. The niche that enabled the B50s to survive was the lightly laid branch between Madiun and Slahung, a route which was not capable of taking heavier locomotives. A handful of Java's delightful C11 class 2-6-0 tanks, built by Hartmann of Germany, also ran beyond their hundredth year.

These pictures provide a fascinating contrast in centenarian 0-4-2s, which survive in sugar plantation service in far-flung areas of the world.
Above left: The Mañuel Isla Perez Sugar Mills in Cuba operated this Baldwin, which was built in 1882.
Above right: Motipur sugar factory's metre gauge E class No. 3 was built in Britain for the Bombay, Baroda & Central India Railway in 1876–7.

Opposite: A definitive Sharp Stewart at Sabero Colliery in Spain. Named *El Esla*, the veteran was built at the company's Great Bridgewater Street works in Manchester in 1885, two years before Sharp Stewart moved to Glasgow.

CENTENARIANS

The railways of Spain had a wonderful diversity of ancient locomotives, but income derived from tourism in the 1960s was used to modernize the entire railway network. Fortunately, some of the antiquities, in the form of 0-6-0 and 0-8-0 goods engines, gravitated into the country's many collieries to achieve centenarian status. One of these was an 0-8-0 built by Hartmann of Chemnitz in 1879, which survived at the Olloniegro Colliery. This engine – a rare example of a very early 0-8-0 – ran beyond its hundredth year and still lay derelict at Olloniegro into the early 1990s. Spain had yet another centenarian Sharp

Stewart in the form of the delightful *El Esla*, an 0-6-0 tank of 1885, which in 1987 remained hard at work at Sabero Colliery, taking local coal trains down to the RENFE main line connection.

The remaining examples which come to mind are from Latin America. In Brazil, at the Usina Barcelos, a lovely Baldwin 4-4-0 of 1876 topped its hundredth year, while intrepid travellers to Puerto Eten in Peru during the 1970s were rewarded by the sight of a classic American 4-4-0, built in 1870 by Rogers of Paterson, New Jersey, an echo of early railways in the US.

The world's oldest steam survivors were built by Sharp Stewart's Great Bridgewater Street works in Manchester. Both are D class metre gauge 0-4-0 tender engines of 1873; one is named *Tweed* and the other *Mersey*. Both remain active at Indian sugar factories. *Tweed* works at Saraya Sugar Mills and *Mersey* – the engine shown here – at SKG Mills, Hathua. It is depicted in company with two of the mill's 600mm (1ft 11 1/2 in) gauge Baldwin 4-6-0s, originally built for the field railways of World War I.

The smiling face of this American veteran makes an interesting comparison with the British-built Sharp Stewart engine on page 15. It is Cuba's oldest locomotive, having been built by Baldwin in 1878, and is caught here reposing in the shed entrance at the Ruben Martinez Villeña sugar mill.

FINLAND *Scandinavian stronghold of steam*

Above: A rake of sand for permanent way work trundles over the river near Hyrynsalmi behind Finnish State Railway TV1 class No. 921. This picture was taken on 4 April 1972 as winter was releasing its icy grip on the frozen river.

Opposite: Finnish State Railway TV1 class 2-8-0 No. 921 heads a permanent way special through the snow-bound conifer forests of the Kontiomaki to Joensuu line.

FINLAND was once a grand duchy of the Russian Empire, but its railways have followed a distinctly separate development, although the 5ft (1524mm) gauge is common to both.

The distinction of Finnish locomotive designs owes much to the country's indigenous building capacity, which was set up at the beginning of the twentieth century. The two companies – Tampella, located in the city of the same name and known as the 'Manchester of Finland', and Lohono Oy – built the majority of the country's locomotives. Tampella is also famous for the manufacture of linen.

A leading characteristic of the Finnish school was light axleloadings, as huge areas of bog and clay were encountered when the railways were built. An engine's classification reflects this: 'k' being for axle weights of up to 11 tons; 'v' up to 14 tons; and 'r' for weights in excess of 14 tons.

Finland's dark conifer green locomotives and the railway itself blended delightfully with the landscape, which is 70 per cent forest with 60,000 lakes. The railway network had an incredible 8,000 level crossings. Finnish engines traditionally burnt birch logs, creating a distinctive aroma for those accustomed to steam raised by coal or oil, but in the later years a mixture of birch logs and imported Russian coal predominated.

Part of the Finnish State Railway extends over the Arctic Circle into Lapland, where engine cow-catchers are known as reindeer-catchers.

Finland was the last stronghold of steam in Scandinavia and, after all operations had finished in the late 1970s, many engines remained mothballed in the forests as part of a national strategic reserve.

REMNANTS OF THE SPANISH VINTAGE

IN 1965, 35 per cent of Spain's steam locomotives were over fifty years old and engines of 80, 90 and even 100 years were not uncommon. Within 10 years this situation had changed dramatically: the jet age had launched the sun-soaked package holidays, and with it Spain found a new industry. The money gained from tourism was wisely used to modernize the nation's crumbling infrastructure and the railway was a principal recipient. By the late 1970s Spain was no longer the treasure house of vintage steam, but remnants survived and examples of the legacy lingered on into the 1990s.

Spain has a wonderful tradition of pensioning off old main line locomotives into industrial service, and many 0-6-0s, 0-8-0s and tank engines have achieved centenarian status in this way.

Perhaps the most amazing success was the former Northern Railway 0-8-0 No. 2151, built by Hartmann of Chemnitz in 1879. Named *El Cavado* after the Spanish river, it was pensioned off to coalfield service and was active for over 100 years. It remained dumped at Olloniego into the 1990s. This amazing engine must have been one of the world's first 0-8-0s.

On the Tharsis Sulphur & Copper Company, Dübs 0-4-0 saddle tank No. 1 *Odiel* of 1867 remained derelict in 1987 – 120 years later, while a Dübs 0-6-0 tank of 1881 lies marooned on a ledge following a landslide on the Rio Tinto system.

Not all the centenarians are derelict: at Sabero Colliery an 0-6-0 tank named *El Esla* was still hard at work in the early 1990s, having been built by Sharp Stewart at their Great Bridgewater Street works in Manchester in 1885. In contrast another Manchester classic exists in Industrias Lopez's scrapyard in Zaragoza in the form of an 0-6-0 tank built at Beyer Peacock's Gorton works in 1875.

A scene at the coal screens at Sabero colliery with metre gauge 0-4-0 tank No. 5 *Vego Barrio*. This locomotive worked turn-about with the 1885-built Sharp Stewart 0-6-0 tank *El Esla* and is believed to be of Couillet extraction. The picture was taken on 18 March 1987.

This beautiful locomotive is one of a rare breed known as 'scrap tanks' – locomotives which have been built locally from the remains of older engines which have been broken up. This is a 2-4-0 tank working on the 5ft 6in (1676mm) gauge metals on the Turon complex which formed part of the Hunosa colliery group in northern Spain. Numbered 103, it was allegedly put together at Turon in 1921, but the origin of the parts is unknown. The picture was taken on 5 April 1971.

DOMINANT FOR TWO DECADES *The Atlantics*

Left: Great Northern Large Atlantic No. 256 on a northbound express. These attractive engines were built between 1902 and 1910. Until the advent of larger locomotives in the 1920s, GN Atlantics hauled the crack expresses from London to York. These locomotives epitomize the elegance of the steam era. The last of the class was withdrawn in 1950, and the railway fraternity mourned their passing. Below: The world's last Atlantics ran in Mozambique, having been built by Henschel of Germany in 1925. They were built for the Nampula line, and here No. 814 shunts on to the pier at Lumbo in 1969.

Britain's North Eastern Railway made extensive use of Atlantics in various guises. Here a Class Z1 is 'caught' in company with a monoplane during the early years of the twentieth century. This must have been a composite picture, celebrating the latest technology of the day.

BY 1900, the 4-4-2 wheel arrangement, known as Atlantic, had rendered the large-wheeled express passenger 4-4-0 out of date for fast passenger services on America's railroads. The Atlantic's power, generated from the larger firebox that the trailing bogie was added to carry, made the type excellent both for heavy trains at medium speeds and for sustained fast running with moderately loaded trains. For express use, Atlantics were given driving wheels as large as 7ft in diameter. The speed of the Atlantic was emphasized by the Pennsylvania Railroad's insistence that one of their engines reached a speed of 127 mph (203km/h) – a claim that was taken seriously by many railway authorities in America.

However, the Atlantic was absent from Russia, where the Prairie was widely adopted, nor did the Atlantic find much favour in Latin America, China or in most of Africa. But the Atlantic's era is a celebrated part of the railway history of America, France and Britain. By the 1920s, the appearance of steel coaches had increased train weights, especially in America, while expresses were getting heavier the world over. The Atlantic was the intermediate stage between the 4-4-0 and the 4-6-0, which was the next logical phase of development, becoming the principal express passenger type for many areas of the world until the end of steam.

Curiously, the last Atlantics left in service anywhere in the world were a class of Henschel-built examples belonging to the Caminhos de Ferro de Moçambique (Mozambique State Railways). These handsome machines, complete with smoke deflectors, were in everyday use until as late as 1975. The civil war in the country meant that few photographs were taken of them.

A good number of Atlantics have been preserved, but very few are in working condition.

AMERICAN CLASSICS IN CUBA

A twilight scene at the Carlos Mañuel de Cespedes sugar mill in Cuba.
The engine is an 0-4-0 saddle tank built by Baldwin of Philadelphia in 1916.
It has been converted to burn oil which is carried in the additional
rectangular tank on the running plate, so providing an additional source of
adhesion for heavy movements around the yard.

CUBA is a veritable treasure house of classic American steam. Before Fidel Castro's revolution of 1959, the country was in essence under American colonial rule, and this is reflected in the island's railways. Castro's Communist administration brought a swift and hostile reaction from the US, and a trade embargo has existed since the days of President Kennedy – an act that has left Cuba's locomotives 'frozen in time'. Although steam has disappeared from the Cuban State Railway's main lines, it survives in great variety on the railway networks of many of the island's sugar mills. Sugar lies at the heart of Cuba's economy, and of a total of some 150 mills, around one-third uses steam traction.

Cuba's locomotives are all oil-burners, the island having no indigenous coal, and most of the locomotives are of main line proportions. The sugar trains are heavily loaded, many of them work over long distances, which in some cases involve running over the Cuban main line network to reach the outlying cane fields.

The cane-harvesting season is from February to April, a time of frenzied activity with round-the-clock operations. The nine-month lay-off period then provides ample time for maintenance and the skilful 'make-do-and-mend', which has enabled the veteran locomotives to be kept going against all odds.

It is an unforgettable sight to see a vintage Baldwin 2-8-0 hauling a heavy sugar cane train over steep gradients, the experience heightened by the sonorous whistles, the ringing of warning bells, and wooden-bodied signal-boxes on stilts, all so evocative of American railroad practice during the steam age.

Detailed studies from locomotives active on Cuba's sugar mills. The smokebox door plate bearing the number 1711 is carried by Alco Cook 2-8-0 No. 62099, built in September 1920. 'Venceremos' refers to Cuban revolutionary zeal and means 'we shall overcome'; the engine works at the Boris Luis Santa Coloma sugar mill. This cab-side detail of No. 1104 is typical of many embellishments on Cuban locomotives. It belongs to a Baldwin 0-4-0 saddle tank working at the E.G. Lavandero Mill.

One of Cuba's most powerful locomotive types are these 19XX class medium-range 2-8-0s. Here No. 1907, a Baldwin engine of July 1924, brings a heavy drag of cane in from the plantations to the Carlos Mañuel de Cespedes sugar mill in Camaguey Province.

Cuba is the world's last bastion of classic American steam, and here a classic wooden signal-box on stilts protects the flat crossing at Robles. Baldwin Mogul No. 53822, built in January 1920, completes the scene.

THE ULTIMATE IN AMERICAN STEAM

THE Mallet articulated was to find its forte in the United States, as did the Garratt in Africa. The US had no place for the Garratt, whilst few large Mallets ever ran in Africa.

America's first Mallet was the Baltimore & Ohio's giant 0-6-6-0 four-cylinder compound known as *Old Maud*, which made her debut at the World Fair Exposition in St Louis in 1904. She was a classic Mallet: her two high-pressure cylinders drove the rear engine and the pivoted front engine was driven by the two low-pressure cylinders. Although *Maud* was not successful in line service, the precedent had been created, and an 0-8-8-0 and 2-8-8-0 Mallet type followed. In 1906 the Great Northern received a 2-6-6-2 Mallet from Baldwin.

Mallets for line service had leading trucks for stability; those without found extensive use in the hump shunting yards, where massive tonnages had to be heaved up steep slopes to allow the wagons to roll under their own momentum. The Mallet spread to many US railroads. They were superb for slogging hauls though the Rockies and for the massive drags from coalfields. By 1911, the Santa Fe had aspired to an incredible 2-10-10-2 Mallet. The Mallet was almost exclusively fitted with medium-sized driving wheels, allowing a massive firebox to be built above them for adequate steam generation.

The 2-8-8-2 type became favourite both for its potential low axle weights – often little more than a Mikado for double the power available. Alternatively, if the track and bridges were strong enough, the 2-8-8-2 could aspire to massive proportions.

After the mid-1920s, the Mallet was developed as a simple rather than a compound in order to achieve faster line speeds, and many compounds were converted to simples.

The Challenger 4-6-6-4 simple introduced in 1936 was a massive advance; its stability and top speed of 70mph (112km/h) enabled it to be used on passenger trains. The ultimate was reached with the Union Pacific's famous 7,000hp 4-8-8-4 simple 'Big Boys' of 1944. These were the largest and heaviest steam locomotives ever built, at 520 tons in full working order. These and their contemporary relation, the 2-6-6-6 Alleghenies, represented the ultimate development of steam power before research turned to other forms of traction.

Above: The solitary Pennsylvania Railroad's Duplex S1 No. 6100 was the biggest and heaviest non-articulated passenger locomotive ever built. It was exhibited at the New York World Fair, having been built at the Pennsylvania Railroad's works at Altoona in 1939. It had a working life of only eight years and was scrapped in 1949, its line of evolution being cut short by advancing dieselization.

Opposite: It would be hard to surpass the Union Pacific's 4-8-8-4 or 'Big Boy' for sheer size and power. These locomotives were built to handle freight trains over the mountains between Wyoming and Utah. The sight of one of these at the head of a 3,600-ton freight must have been awesome.

LEGACY OF A CHEQUERED HISTORY

POLISH narrow gauge operations were one of the last bright spots of European steam. By the 1980s, by far the most common type to survive was the ubiquitous 750mm (2ft 5½in) gauge PX48, a 40-ton standard design from the Polish builder Chrzanow. Before the introduction of the PX48, Poland's narrow gauge lines were operated by dozens of older designs, predating the nation's re-emergence as a free state after World War I.

Many of these lines had begun as German military railways, and the motive power inherited was diverse, as were the gauges. Some PX48s were regauged to work on 785mm (2ft 6¾in) and metre gauge (3ft 3⅜in) lines. Another prevalent Polish locomotive type was the KP4s, an 0-8-0 built during the 1950s, primarily for export.

Many Polish industries have been served by narrow gauge lines: sugar factories, coal mines, steel works, stone quarries, gravel pits and forestry systems. Poland's 750mm forestry railway at Czarna Bialostocka was a 75-mile (120km) long route which was host to the last German Feldbahns – the standard field locomotive for military operations during World War I.

Sadly, by the mid-1980s, the Polish State Railways had embarked on a policy of dieselization on the surviving narrow gauge lines, although steam was preferred by many of the operators. The boilers of narrow gauge locomotives were in demand for industrial use, and today little is left of one of Europe's most fascinating networks.

Left: Two abandoned Feldbahns on the Czarna Bialostocka system. On the left is TX class No. 227 bearing a plate 'Esslingen 1916' and on the right TX class No. 201, built by Borsig of Berlin in 1918.
Above: A derelict Feldbahn TX class No. 1123 bearing a Hohenzollern of Düsseldorf plate lies dumped in primeval woods in Hajnowka in May 1983.
Right: The last surviving Feldbahn TX class No. 1117, built by Henschel of Kassel in 1918 as works No. 15973, is caught rolling though the woods on the Czarna Bialostocka system on 23 May 1983.

SUPREME FOR THIRTY YEARS *Classic British 4-4-0's*

FROM the time of its inception with the Highland Railway's Jones Goods type in 1894, the 4-6-0 was destined to play a prominent role in the development of fast passenger and freight locomotives. Curiously Britain had been exporting 4-6-0s for some years before David Jones caused a sensation by introducing the formative wheel arrangement on the Highland Railway, which had seldom been in the headlines. During the Edwardian period, 4-6-0s also became active on the Great Western, Caledonian and Great Central railways. The last included in its roster a class designated 'Fish Engines' for fish trains timed to run at passenger train speeds between the docks at Grimsby and London.

Until the widespread adoption of the Pacific during the 1930s, the 4-6-0 was, for the first 30 years of the twentieth century, the principal express passenger type, either in the form of four-cylinder engines, like the Great Western Stars, Castles and Kings and the London & North Western Claughton, or three-cylinder types, like the London Midland & Scottish Royal Scots and the Southern Railway's Lord Nelsons. These were ultimately eclipsed by the Pacific on all but the Great Western. However, from the mid-1930s, the 4-6-0 became increasingly developed in the form of powerful two-cylinder mixed-traffic types. Pre-eminent in this category were Stanier's Black 5s on the LMS, which eventually totalled 842 engines, Thompson's B1s for the London & North Eastern, totalling 410 examples, and the Great Western's Halls and Granges, which together also totalled 410 examples.

The situation was perpetuated by British Railways, formed by nationalization of the 'Big Four' in 1948, with the Standard 5 4-6-0s, which were based on the extremely successful LMS Black 5s; 171 examples were built between 1951 and 1957, along with 80 lighter Standard 4s for more general duties.

Opposite: The Southern Railway's Lord Nelson class would perform well in the hands of an experienced crew. No. 858 *Lord Duncan* is shown speeding a rake of Pullmans bound for 'the smoke'.

Above: One of Bowen Cooke's magnificent four-cylinder Claughton 4-6-0s, introduced in 1913 as the principal express passenger type for the London & North Western Railway. During their later years, 20 of the class received larger boilers like the example shown here. The engine depicted is No. 5946 *Duke of Connaught*, seen at Chester in LMS days.

STEAM ON THE VELDT

SOUTH African Railways became world famous during the early 1970s. Apart from being one of the world's last great steam users, the country had a wonderful variety of types working amid glorious landscapes with the perfect climate for photography. Some of the classic nineteenth-century types, like the Scottish-built Class 6 4-6-0 and Class 7 4-8-0, which had elegant Victorian/Edwardian lines, survived in industrial service until 1980.

In common with North America, South African motive power evolved rapidly. The country was rich in natural resources and, as the economy grew, ever-larger and more powerful types were needed to haul the increasingly heavy trains over difficult terrain, compounded by often cheaply laid track and heavy grades. The 2-8-2 appeared in 1903 and by 1906 4-8-2s were in operation.

The move to Mallet power came in 1910 in the form of 2-6-6-0s and later 2-6-6-2s. But the Mallet was destined to conquer the United States, and it was the articulated Garratt that became the firm favourite in South Africa, following its introduction there in 1920. The Garratt was perfect for South African conditions and culminated in some extremely potent designs like the GMA 4-8-2+2-8-4 that could climb gradients of 1 in 40. These engines had a massive tractive effort of 68,800lb (31,208kg) and an axleloading of less than 15 tons.

In retrospect, 1925 was a watershed: the arrival of American-built Class15CB 4-8-2s and Class16D Pacifics marked a departure from the previous reliance on contemporary British thinking for motive power design. The stage was set for the introduction of the Class 15F and 23 4-8-2s, which were two of the nation's non-

Above: A Class 12A 4-8-2 enjoys a further lease of life on the Witbank Colliery network in the Transvaal.
Opposite: The flooded waters of the tidal Swartzkops River in Port Elizabeth mirror a suburban train from Uitenhage headed by a North British-built Class 16 CR Pacific.

With the prospect of heavy rain in the offing, a Class 19D of the South African Railways hauls an express across the Veldt.

Steam on the veldt

Below: South African Railways 25NC class 4-8-4 Gerda heads a 20-coach Kimberly to De Aar stopping train in 1990. These engines were unofficially named after girls by the depot that operated them. The names of girlfriends, wives and daughters were carried on plates bolted on the smokebox door.

Right: The weekly Orange Express, headed by the solitary South African Railway's Red Devil 4-8-4 heads through Kraankkuil on its journey from Kimberly to De Aar in 1990. The Orange Express changed to diesel haulage in 1986, but reverted to steam in 1989, and over the following few years was worked by Kimberly 25NC 4-8-4s with the Red Devil making intermittent appearances on this working, as it was a Kimberly engine at this time.

articulated standard types until the end of steam.

Superpower was reached with the mighty condensing 4-8-4s of 1953. These were a Henschel design for working trains through the arid Karroo Desert. Their total weight in full working order was 234 tons and total length 108 feet (33m) — their enormously long tenders carrying the condensing elements. These locomotives were amongst the most fascinating of latter-day steam designs. A non-condensing version classified 25NC appeared in 1954.

The 25NCs were amongst the most flamboyant of latter-day steam giants and survived until the end of South African steam. A handful still see occasional use, and during the winter of 1997–8 oil-fired No. 3501 was on shunting duties at Beaconsfield and even some line work.

There was passionate world-wide interest in the perpetuation of steam in South Africa, and this gave rise to an heroic attempt to make improvements and economies to the traditional locomotive. The result was the unique Red Devil, which was a rebuilt 25NC 4-8-4. It was designed by David Wardale incorporating the principles of the celebrated Argentinean locomotive engineer L.D. Porta. Sadly the tide of feeling against steam was so powerful that this bold development came to nothing.

Fireless locomotives

THE concept of a steam locomotive with a 'fire in its belly' is a universal allure. The Fireless, however, has no such animation, being more akin to a thermos flask on wheels. For those industries with a ready supply of high-pressure steam, it has been widely celebrated as the most efficient and economical shunting engine ever devised. Running costs are minimal, largely because the heavy stresses of a firebox are absent, and of course only a driver, is required.

The principle behind the fireless is that steam is injected at high pressure into a storage vessel and then fed to the cylinders through a reducing valve to achieve constant power output before a recharge becomes necessary. Although Fireless locomotives have been used in many industries, they are particularly relevant in establishments where sparks from a conventional engine could wreak havoc, such as munitions factories, paper mills and jute mills.

In spite of their undeniable efficiency, so great has been the witch hunt against steam traction that even the dependable Fireless, with all its in-built simplicity and longevity, has passed into extinction in most parts of the world. However, a number of fascinating examples – some very powerful – do still survive throughout Europe, especially in the former East Germany, where examples were still being built as late as the 1980s.

If there is an indictment to be made against the Fireless, it is its occasional tendency to run out of steam at the opposite end of the system from where the works' boilers are situated.

Opposite: Cuba has some rare Baldwin-built Fireless locomotives, and here No.1169, a Baldwin 0-4-0 built in September 1917, is caught undertaking its work-a-day chores at the Bolivia Sugar Mill in Camaguey Province.

Right: Fireless engines were found at many British industrial establishments. A German innovation, the Fireless was taken up by Andrew Barclay in Kilmarnock in 1913, and appeared in many facets of British industry until dying out during the early 1970s, as part of the national obsession to be rid of steam traction.

Below: This Andrew Barclay 0-4-0 Fireless was built in 1956 and is seen working at the Imperial Paper Mill at Gravesend, Kent. Although extinct in most parts of the world, an interesting range of Fireless engines – some of them powerful machines – survive in various European industries.

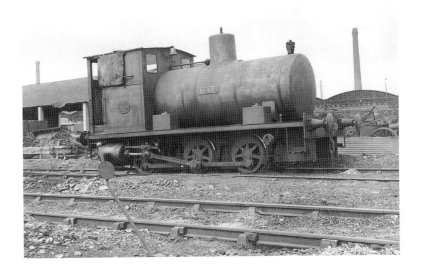

RIDING THE IRON HORSE *Steam in the blood*

FEW professions have had so many admirers as the steam locomotive driver; the concept of being in control of a 200-ton locomotive and physically sensing the surging power at the touch of one's fingers is a thrilling idea by any standards.

The spirit was beautifully revealed in a British television programme transmitted in April 1998. The film showed vintage footage of Driver Joseph Duddington and Fireman T.H. Bray, the crew of *Mallard*, on that fateful day, 3 July 1938, when they achieved the world speed record for steam of 126mph (201.6km/h). The pride of these men and their devotion to the job and the company, as well as their respect for the locomotive, were obvious.

In many respects, the steam locomotive bought out the best in men. Unlike diesel or electric traction, a steam locomotive had to be nurtured, and in order to give of its best called upon the skill of its crew. Every steam locomotive was different, an individual in its own right which crews had to get to know to extract the best performance.

Of course it was hard toil, full of discomforts, especially for the fireman, who had to shovel tons of coal across a swaying footplate. Engines were hot in summer and cold in winter, and many were wet when it rained. The dust, the glare, the noise were all factors set against steam by advocates of modernization. But for all the vicissitudes of life on the footplate, drivers and firemen were deeply attached to their work and the steam locomotive.

Above: A locomotive driver on an Indian Railways' 2ft 6in (762mm) gauge ZB class Pacific on the Pulgaon–Arvi line. Opposite: A cab interior on a Baldwin 2-8-0 at the E.G. Lavandero sugar mill in Cuba. The engine is an oil-burner and the jets have been turned on fully to raise steam to full pressure.

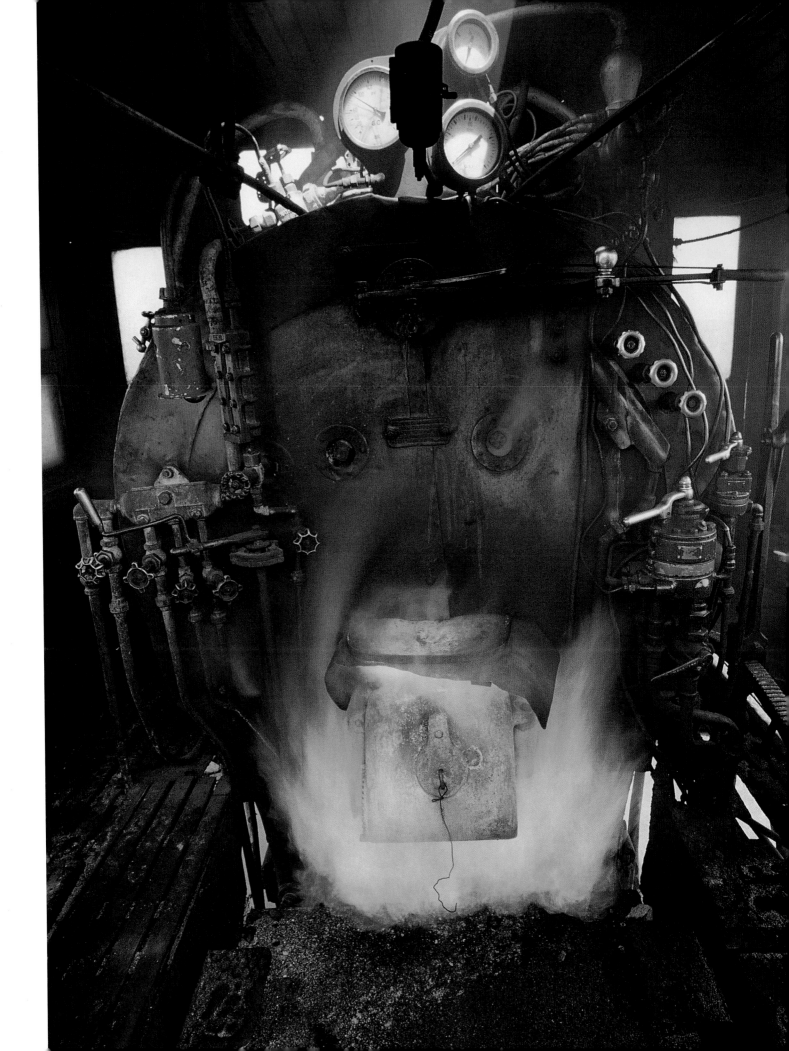

ARTERIES OF INDUSTRY

NARROW gauge railways were once the arteries of industry, enabling railways to serve virtually all aspects of industrial development – not least railway building itself. Plantations of all kinds, especially sugar and timber, iron and steel works, collieries, stone and slate quarries, iron-ore mines, docks and harbours, shipyards, factories, railway works, gasworks, electricity generating stations and many other installations all featured narrow gauge steam systems, in varying degrees, around the world. They also played a role in warfare, whether bringing supplies up to the front line or trundling rakes of munitions around an armaments factory.

Many were essentially farmers' lines, bringing produce – and invariably passengers – to connect with main line systems in the blissful days before the motor car ended the deep quiet of rural landscapes. The idiosyncracies of the rural steam train were summed up by the words on a locally produced postcard featuring a train on the Wantage Tramway. Although this was a standard gauge line it epitomized the essence of the narrow gauge country railway, and the postcard detailed an alleged race between the train and a local chimney sweep's cart. It was captioned thus:

> *An amazing race has come to pass*
> *Between an engine and an ass,*
> *The Wantage train all steam and smoke*
> *Was beat by Arthur Hitchcock's moke.*

Europe and Asia had the most narrow gauge railways, and they were important in many parts of Africa and Latin America. Their significance in the US depended very much on the area of the country: they were crucial to the mining and logging operations of Colorado, for example, but in the heavily industrialized states, railway operations within plants tended to be standard gauge, linked to the various railroad companies.

The finest narrow gauge lines survive today in Cuba, where a variety of gauges remains in operation on the island's sugar plantations. Other systems are active on the sugar plantations of Java, Sumatra, India and to a lesser extent the Philippines. There is even a single forestry system in Pakistan, near Lahore. China's 750mm (2ft 5½in) gauge forestry systems, though declining, still offer much of interest, although the motive power is relatively standardized with 0-8-0 tender engines.

Above: One of the world's remotest narrow gauge industrial systems, which survived until as recently as the late 1990s, was the coalfield of Upper Assam in north-eastern India (see page 136) where 2ft (610mm) gauge Bagnall saddle tanks were supplemented with redundant engines from the Darjeeling Himalayan Railway. Here, a former Darjeeling veteran enjoys a further lease of active life at Tipong Colliery. The 0-4-0 saddle tank, built by North British of Glasgow in 1914, was photographed in November 1976.

Opposite: An Alfred County Railway train from Harding leaves Bongwana hauled by two NGG16A class 2-6-2+2-6-2 Garratts. These 2ft (610mm) gauge engines were introduced in 1937; most were built by Beyer Peacock (hence Beyer Garratt), but the final batch – the last Garratts to be built – were delivered from Hunslet Taylor in Leeds as late as 1967–8, after Beyer Peacock's demise.

EARLY AMERICAN CLASSIC *Outside cylinder 4-4-0's*

Top left: The classic American 4-4-0 was famous throughout the world for its role in countless films about the American continent, such as *The General*.
Top right: The Swedish Class C 4-4-0 proved to be a highly successful locomotive, so much so, that over 70 were built between 1892 and 1903.
Above: A Southern Railway Schools class in pre-war livery waits to depart from a London terminal at the head of an express for the south coast.

BY far the most dramatic manifestation of the outside cylinder 4-4-0 was the balloon-stacked American examples. These were the principal form of locomotive during the early years of railroading in the US and the type is known as the 'American'. The adherence to outside cylinders was the result of the metallurgy of the time being insufficiently advanced to fabricate crank axles without a high risk of breakages.

The other principal 4-4-0 user was Britain, where the type was not developed until the last quarter of the nineteenth century. By this time, crank axles were a practical proposition, and as America standardized on outside-cylinder 4-4-0s, Britain almost exclusively developed inside-cylinder ones, resulting in some of the prettiest locomotives ever built.

The 4-4-0 appeared in many areas of the world. In general, engines exported from the US had outside cylinders while those from Britain were inside connected, each nation mirroring its home practice. The Prussian State Railways used outside-cylinder 4-4-0s, because their compound expansion created too large a cylinder to fit inside the frames. Interestingly, in the case of Britain's three-cylinder Midland compounds, the two high-pressure cylinders were placed outside and the larger low-pressure one was inside.

The railways of the former Dutch East Indies had one of the most fascinating colLections of motive power of any country in the world. Amongst them was a class of 44 compound 4-4-0s built between 1900 and 1909 by three manufacturers – Hanomag, Hartmann and Werkspoor. B5117 was photographed at Babat shed in August 1975.

DRAMATIC INDUSTRIAL PERFORMERS
Slag-tipping engines

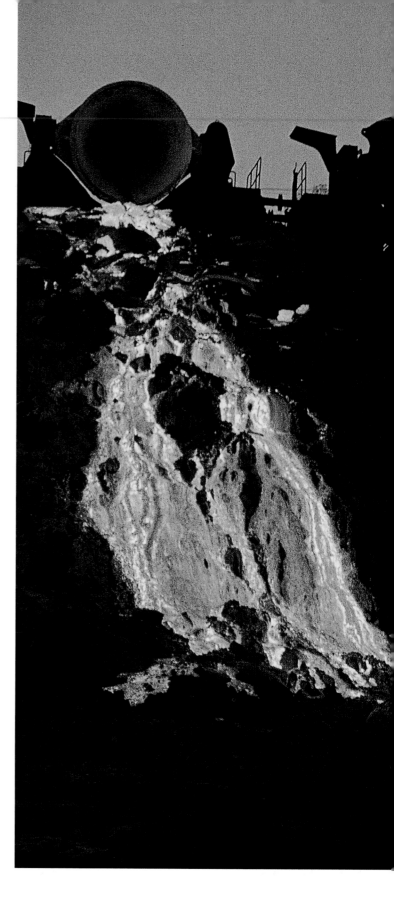

TIPPING molten waste from blast furnaces, down what is known as the 'slag bank', was one of the great dramas of the Industrial Revolution, especially when enacted with steam locomotives. Such sights were once common throughout the industrialized world, and at night whole towns would be illuminated by the ghastly flares. Today, there are only a handful of places on earth where this industrial drama of a bygone age can still be witnessed.

Slag is primarily rock and soil separated from the iron in the blast furnaces. The waste is poured in a liquid form into ladle wagons to be conveyed by rail to the slag bank, which is usually situated on the periphery of the works. Ideally, the waste should be molten when tipped, but if delays occur in transit it solidifies, necessitating manual hammering on the upturned cauldrons to dislodge it.

Imagine the whirr of ropes, the creaking of an upturned cauldron, the cataclysmic blaze of light and the hideous crackle as the waste explodes upon hitting the ground. From a molten river, terrifying fingers pour into every nook and cranny. Slag banks resemble the mountains of the moon and are an excellent source of aggregate for building foundations. However, in recent years, it has proved more economical to discharge the molten waste into artificial lakes. This changes the chemical balance and renders the slag suitable for cement manufacture. Though less spectacular, the hot slag emptied into cold water causes a blast of steam to shoot skywards like an atomic explosion

Slag tipping by night at Turkey's Karabuk steelworks, set amid mountainous country near the Black Sea coast. The engine is a standard Hawthorn Leslie type 0-6-0 saddle tank and is one of a batch delivered to Turkey, both from Hawthorn Leslie and Robert Stephenson & Hawthorn following the merger of the two companies in 1937.

VETERAN LOCOMOTIVES OF WORLD WAR I

RAILWAYS have played a prolific part in war operations ever since the Crimea campaign of 1854. They have been essential for the movements of supplies and troops, no more so than during World War I when hundreds of miles of narrow gauge track reached up to the front lines.

Inevitably special locomotives were designed for these operations, and they were built in such large numbers that they became among the best-known types in world history.

On the standard gauge, J.G. Robinson's Great Central 2-8-0s of 1911 were chosen by the Ministry of Defence, along with the Great Western Dean Goods 0-6-0, both types seeing widespread service overseas.

However, on the 600mm (1ft 11⅝ in) field railways, special designs were prepared, and on the Allied side Hunslet of Leeds produced a 4-6-0 tank in 1915. However, owing to the pressures of other wartime work, Hunslet could not produce them in sufficient numbers so Baldwin of America came to the rescue with a substitute 4-6-0 tank, 495 of which were built in 1916–17. These were followed by 100 2-6-2 tanks from Alco. These proved especially popular, and following the cessation of hostilities both types were surplus to military requirements; many passed into industrial service, including some batches which went to the sugar fields of British India.

On the German side the standard Prussian designs fulfilled requirements on the standard gauge, while the field railways were ably worked by the Feldbahn, one of the most celebrated war engines – 2,500 were in service by 1919, the products of at least 11 different builders. Many Feldbahns also passed into industrial service following the war.

Left: Some of the American-built 600mm (1ft 11⅝ in) tank engines survived another 60 years in industrial service, like this Baldwin 4-6-0 at the Upper India Sugar Mills, at Khatauli in 1981.
Opposite: A German Feldbahn on the forestry system at Czarna Bialostocka in north-eastern Poland, close to the Russian border. The Feldbahns at this location were the last to remain in service, and survived until the mid-1980s.

VETERAN LOCOMOTIVES OF WORLD WAR II

Left: Between 7,000 and 8,000 Kriegslok, or war locos, were built during World War II to supply the German military machine with a viable, efficient form of motive power. These simple-to-maintain but rugged engines lasted until the end of steam. In this painting, a tired work-weary example rests amid the gloom of a running shed.

Below: A metre gauge McArthur Mikado lies at Acladokampos in the Greek Peloponnese.

Opposite: One of Major Marsh's classic S160 2-8-0s departs from Liankladion station with a freight bound for Athens on Saturday 20 April 1973. These engines were active in Greece until 1976.

THE use of railways during World War II between 1939 and 1945 extended to numerous fronts over many parts of the world: Europe, the Middle East, North Africa and the Far East. As in World War I, many classes of locomotive evolved specifically for war-related traffic.

The most famous type was the standard gauge German Kriegslokomotiv 2-10-0; this was a wartime austerity variant of the Deutsche Reichsbahn's standard Class 50, and some 6,300 were built to follow the German armies in their attempted conquest of Europe and Russia.

The 2-8-0 remained predominant for the allies' standard gauge operations: firstly in the form of Stanier's 8F 2-8-0s, the standard freight engine of the LMS, and latterly in the form of an Austerity version built by North British and Vulcan Foundry in 1944–5. The Ministry of Supply also introduced Britain's first 2-10-0 with 150 Austerities from North British. These were designed to have a lower axleloading than the 2-8-0s, while retaining

their ability to negotiate sharp curves thanks to the centre coupled wheels being flangeless.

The US's powerful standard gauge contribution was also a 2-8-0 in the form of Major Marsh's S160s, which were built to the British loading gauge and were built to the dimensions of Stanier's LMS 8Fs. Well over 2,000 of these stalwarts were produced by Alco, Baldwin and Lima for service in western Europe. Various classes of 0-6-0 tank engine were built in Britain and the US. Metre gauge operations in the Far Eastern theatre were ably covered by the McArthur Mikados. These came from Baldwin and Davenport and went to India, Burma and the Philippines.

The dispersal of war engines, either though military action or post-conflict dispersals, is one of the most fascinating aspects of locomotive history, and some designs like the Kriegsloks, S160s and the McArthur Mikados, have become as close to an international standard design as has ever been achieved.

Opposite: Some of Britain's Ministry of Supply 2-10-0s of 1943 ended up in Greece after the war, and one is caught here simmering at the engine sheds in Alexandropolis.

Above: A United States Army Transportation Corps 0-6-0 tank on duty at Anshan, the iron and steel capital of China. Anshan works retained several of these engines for operating in parts of the complex where access was restricted. Examples survived at Anshan until the early 1990s. Classified XK2, the engine, No. 51, is depicted at steel mill No. 3 on 4 September 1985.

A 1930s STREAMLINED SUPERSTAR *The Hiawatha*

THE 'Hiawatha' was the most exciting of all the high-speed super streamliners which graced the world's railways during the 1930s. A classic product of the streamline era, the inspiration for the 'Hiawatha' was the competition for the daytime rail service between Chicago and the twin cities of St Paul and Minneapolis. The service was initially worked by Atlantics whose streamlining was created by the artist-designer Otto Kuhler. They were oil-fired and built by the American Locomotive Company of Schenectady, New York, and introduced to the Chicago Milwaukee, St Paul & Pacific Railroad in 1935.

The Hiawathas, with their 7ft (213cm) diameter driving wheels, 69sq ft (6.4m²) grate area and 300lb/sq in (21kg/cm²) boiler pressure, were able to develop more than 3,000 horsepower and achieve 110mph (176km/h). It has even been suggested that on a trial run a speed of 128mph (204km/h) was reached. Originally intended to haul six cars on the 431-mile (689km) long water-level route in the 6½-hour schedule, such was their power that they ultimately hauled nine cars in 6½ hours. What made these speeds even more remarkable was that the schedules included five intermediate stops and no less than fifteen sections where there were speed restrictions of below 50mph (80km/h). This meant, that in order to maintain schedule, the journey had to include stretches in which speeds of over 100mph (160km/h) had to be maintained. They were the fastest scheduled steam trains ever to run, and in 1940 the eastbound 'Morning Hiawatha' achieved a world steam record start-to-stop, when it made the 78½-mile (125.6km) run from Sparta to Portage, Wisconsin at an average speed of 81½ mph (130.4km/h).

The Hiawatha waits to leave the terminal at Milwaukee in this fine period picture taken in the late 1930s. The engine is one of the high-speed Atlantics specially built for the service in 1936.

What a sight this must have been! Introduced in the mid-1930s, the streamlined 4-4-2 hauled the 'Hiawatha' between Chicago and St Paul at an average speed of over 80mph (128km/h). Four Atlantic streamliners were built for the Milwaukee Road specifically for the 412-mile (660km) run between the two cities.

LOCOMOTIVE GRAVEYARDS

WORKING steam around the world is now down to about 6,000 locomotives, although thousands more exist in various categories of inactivity or preservation. Most of the silenced locomotives will never work again, but their status varies. Some, especially in industrial service, are held in reserve to diesel or electric traction. Others are stored surplus to immediate requirements, awaiting a decision on their future. In some countries, steam is brought into use for seasonal traffic, such as sugar cane. A few countries have a strategic reserve for use in the event of national or fuel crises – a category which applies to Russia and some of the countries of the former Soviet Union.

Although engines are usually broken up within a year or so of being withdrawn, others can languish for up to 20 or 30 years. In countries where no steel industry exists, the costs of recovering the metals for export can exceed the going rate for scrap. The dumps in which they lie are soon overgrown places, especially in the tropics. Rusting locomotives are quickly covered in creeper and sometimes disappear altogether from sight, requiring a machete to discover their identity. Because so few people visit these sites, they become natural havens for wildlife – wherever there is rusting metal wild flowers seem to abound.

For the locomotive historian these graveyards are rich hunting grounds, occasionally yielding the discovery of a certain type which was long thought to be extinct. In the absence of any plates to make a certain identification, intrepid archaeologists of the steam locomotive resort to scraping the metal for engraved numerals. As the age of steam fades into history, the number of 'well-matured' graveyards has inevitably declined, but individual locomotives, or small groups of them, can be found throughout the world. A few of these have now passed beyond official ownership and lie rotting in no-man's land. Some seem destined to become permanently rotting monuments to a bygone industrial age.

Below left: The locomotive graveyards of the Greek mainland and the Peloponnese were one of the most exotic in the world. Here a moribund metre gauge Z class 2-6-0 tank, which dates back to the 1890s, lies abandoned at Kalamata.

Opposite: The finest locomotive graveyard in Greece was at Salonika in the north of the country where up to 80 historic locomotives could be found until the mid-1980s. The most interesting was at the old station yard where this Gölsdorf-derived simple version of his 0-10-0 of 1900 lay. The Greek State railways ordered these from StEG in Vienna during the mid-1920s, classifying them Kb. Note the ladybird on the flower.

Following pages: Derelict engines are found at many sites in Cuba. Here a 2-8-0 of 1919, built by the American Locomotive Company of Schenectady, and complete with traditional wooden buffer beam, languishes next to another Alco product, an 0-6-0 tank built in 1916 for the United Railways of Havana, though built at Brooks Works rather than Schenectady.

Saxon Meyer 0-4-4-0 No. 99.1606-5 on the now closed line between Wolkenstein and Johstadt. Trains on this picturesque line were often full of walkers using the railway to reach the lovely country through which it passed, sometimes requiring two locomotives to haul the train. Attempts are being made to reopen the line.

One of the world's finest narrow gauge railways operated out of Damascus as far as Sergayah on the Lebanese border. Until the troubles in Lebanon, this line linked Damascus with Beirut by a rack section over the mountains. The line was built to the curious Levantine gauge of 1050mm (3ft 5³⁄₈in). In this scene, taken on 24 June 1976, a 2-6-0 tank, built by SLM at Esslingen in Switzerland, heads an evening passenger train from Sergayah to the Syrian capital.

THE long and characterful tradition of narrow gauge passenger trains is one of endless fascination to both the social historian and railway-lover. In Britain, they were perhaps best characterized by the blissfully rural lines of Col Holman F. Stephens, and in world terms, neatly summed up by Charles Small in his classic book *Far Wheels*, as 'meandering short lines whose antique equipment and leisurely operation were of a relatively unhurried era'.

The world is criss-crossed with derelict narrow gauge lines and very few survive. The last great flowering was in India, where numerous country lines were worked by a plethora of highly varied and individualistic British-built steam engines, whose origins read like a Who's Who of British locomotive builders. Sadly these are but a memory; many have closed and surviving ones are dieselized. The last to succumb was the redoubtable Pulgaon to Arvi line featured on pages 72-5.

Remarkably, the best narrow gauge steam operations in the world today linger on in the former East Germany. When the Berlin Wall fell in 1989, Deutsche Reichsbahn was operating nine narrow gauge lines; all survive today with passengers and some freight. Several of these lines still operate their original steam locomotives, and the rosters vary between 2-10-2 tanks and 0-4-4-0 Mallet tanks. Built to 750mm (2ft 5½in), 900mm (3ft) or metre (3ft 3³⁄₈in) gauges, these lines feature superb scenery, commuter services along with street running and roadside operation. The largest system is the Harzquerbahn in the Harz mountains.

The narrow gauge lines of the former East Germany have mostly survived, and many trains are still steam hauled. The metre gauge Harz system has perhaps the brightest future, hauling tourists as well as locals from Wernigerode up the Brocken – the summit being a cold war listening post. Most trains are hauled by these huge 2-10-2 tanks. No 99.7235-7 approaches Drei Annen Hohne with a Brocken-bound train.

IT is fitting that Britain, the mother country of railways, should have had the most locomotive builders – no less than 350 companies are on record as having constructed locomotives, despite railways having their own workshops.

The primary areas of building and development were centred upon Britain, Europe and the USA. Britain was a prolific supplier of railway equipment throughout her empire and many other areas of the world. A number of European countries received their first locomotives from Britain, but eventually developed their own building capacity, and countries like France, Holland, Belgium, Austria, Germany and Italy all developed export markets.

Around the turn of the century, the huge American builders, having equipped the domestic railroads, began a vigorous and successful export drive to keep their production lines rolling. Baldwin became the world's largest builder, turning out over 70,000 steam locomotives between 1831 and 1953.

The two major land masses of the world that have hardly built any locomotives are Africa and Latin America. China began building relatively late, while Russia developed a vast building industry, later influenced by American practice. The Indian subcontinent relied primarily on imports from Britain until as late as independence in 1947 when, as in many other areas of the world, American influences came to the fore.

The world's principal locomotive builders were either British, European or American; all are represented in this tapestry of builders' plates from steam survivors around the world. Though their factories are no more, these names will live on in the annals of industrial history: names like Beyer Peacock, whose locomotives were noted for their superb workmanship,; or the American Locomotive Company, formed from a variety of builders at the turn of the century.

THE DEMISE OF PAKISTAN'S EDWARDIANS

One of the most remarkable steam survivors of the 1990s were the British inside-cylinder
0-6-0s, which remained active in Pakistan until 1997. Almost identical engines had formed the
mainstay of Britain's freight locomotives a century earlier. The Pakistan Railways examples
were employed on both freight and local passenger work and were converted to oil-burning,
Pakistan having limited indigenous supplies of coal.

Even more remarkable were the Pakistan inside-connected 4-4-0s, which also survived until late 1997. They represent exactly the type of engine which was pre-eminent on express passenger working in Britain during the late Victorian period. Here one of the breed, classified SPS, roars away from the country junction town of Malakwal with a well-loaded train.

ONE of the most fascinating aspects of the world's steam scene was the survival in Pakistan of two definitive forms of British locomotive that characterized the late Victorian and early Edwardian periods: the SPS inside-cylinder 4-4-0 and the SGS inside-cylinder 0-6-0. Their withdrawal at the end of 1997 was a century after almost identical types had been commonplace on the railways of Britain. The mother country was also evoked by the splendid gantries of British semaphore signals, London & North Western-style lever frames and the squeaky London & North Eastern Railway-type whistles of the engines.

It is doubly sad that their demise was not caused through modernization, but rather a general reduction in services on secondary lines. These cuts were imposed as part of the requirements for a World Bank loan. At a time when the West is starting to recognize the futility of road building, Pakistan's government is pressing on with a motorway building programme. Already the air quality in Pakistan's cities is appalling.

Although broad gauge steam in Pakistan has now ended, Moghalpura works in Lahore was continuing to overhaul both SPS and SGS classes during the early months of 1998. It would be difficult to think of a more exciting activity in the world steam scene, although it is uncertain if the locomotives will ever be used.

SINGULARLY BEAUTIFUL *Outstanding express engines*

One of William Dean's famous 2-2-2 locomotives No. 3004 *Black Prince*. The painting shows the locomotive working the 'Cornishman' sometime between the spring of 1892 and the autumn of 1894, when it was rebuilt as a 4-2-2.

THE Single was an express passenger type of high pedigree, and its ultimate flowering led to some of the most beautiful locomotives of all time. Singles were quite unsuited to the rough conditions of the world's emerging railways so they predominated on the well-engineered lines in Europe, especially Britain.

One of the early forms was the 2-2-2s known as the *Jenny Lind* type, built by E. B. Wilson's works in Leeds in 1847. In the same year, Daniel Gooch introduced his maginificent 4-2-2 *Iron Duke*, the first of a class of 31 locomotives, for working the 7ft 0½in (2140mm) broad gauge between Paddington and the West Country. Although 2-2-2s remained in service well into the late nineteenth century, the 4-2-2, with its greater flexibility for fast running, became the preferred type. The large driving wheel diameter of Singles rendered them extremely fleet-footed, and speeds of 90mph (144km/h) were not unusual. However, as trains became increasingly heavy, the Single's lack of adhesion sealed its fate.

Of particular note among Britain's 4-2-2s were Patrick Stirling's Great Northern examples, with 8ft 1in (246cm) diameter wheels, introduced in 1870; Samuel Johnson's Midland Railway Spinners, regarded by many as the most beautiful British locomotive design of all time; and the Caledonian Railway's lovely No. 123, built by Neilson in 1886 for display at that year's International Exhibition of Industry, Science and Arts in Edinburgh.

The final flowering of the Single in Britain came in 1913, when Kerr Stuart of Stoke-on-Trent exported a batch for the flat Kowloon–Canton Railway in China. Their life was almost certainly very short and no pictures of them at work are known to exist.

Above: The Stirling 8ft Single first appeared in 1870, and during the next 23 years 47 were built. Originally, these graceful engines could be seen working the 10am King's Cross–Edinburgh express known in later years as the 'Flying Scotsman'.

Below: LNWR Lady of the Lake class 2-2-2 Single No 802 *Red Gaunlet* in rebuilt form. Some of this class survived on the cross-country Oxford–Bletchley–Cambridge line until the early years of the twentieth century.

KAISERS OF THE TRACKS *Prussian locomotives*

THE Prussian State Railways produced an exciting range of standard designs, some of them in huge numbers. These designs remained in service almost until the end of steam, while Prussian practice exerted a considerable influence on the motive power development of the Reichsbahn following the amalgamation of Germany's railways in 1920.

The most famous Prussian type was the mixed-traffic P8 of 1906. These were the first superheated 4-6-0s, and their success convinced the Prussians (and locomotive engineers elsewhere) that compounding was unnecessary. By the 1930s, 3,850 P8s were in service. Their boiler was common with the G10 0-10-0 heavy freight type, which also numbered more than 3,500 examples.

By far the most numerous Prussian design, however, was the G8 0-8-0 of 1902–13, which, including the G8[1] built from 1913 to 1921, reached the amazing total of 5,087 locomotives. The type saw use in 20 different countries, embracing three continents.

In 1915, Henschel of Kassel prepared a development of the G10 in the form of the G12, a massive three-cylinder 2-10-0, which could haul 1,000-ton trains over 1 in 200 gradients at 25mph (40km/h); 1,500 were built and the type was the forerunner of the Deutsche Reichsbahn's famous Class 44.

In 1919, a smaller version of the G12 was prepared in the form of the $G8^2$; these were 2-8-0s and over 1,000 were built.

Prussian types spread by a combination of German war activity, by territorial changes, and as a result of Germany's vigorous export market. The P8s could be seen working passenger trains in many eastern European countries after World War I reparations made them widespread. Several of these Prussian types rank among the all-time greats in steam locomotive history.

Above: This Prussian G8[2] 2-8-0 was one of 62 examples built for Turkey between 1927 and 1935 from Nohab in Sweden and Tubize in Belgium. This engine was one of a batch which worked the Eregli colliery system on the Black Sea coast, drawing coal from inland collieries to the staithes.
Opposite: Turkish State Railways received numerous Prussian G8 class 0-8-0s and examples lingered on in main line service until the late 1980s. No. 44071 receives attention on 26 June 1987 at Burdur where it was one of the small stud of G8s based for working on secondary routes.

THE Pulgaon to Arvi line was the last steam-worked narrow gauge railway in India (with the exception of two hill station lines on which steam has been kept for historical reasons). It was once part of the Great Indian Peninsular Railway and left its 5 ft 6 in (1676mm) main line at Pulgaon to thread 21 miles (33km) across remote cotton-growing countryside to Arvi. Many of the nine stations on the route, which retains all the characteristics of a classic country railway of the late nineteenth century, are simply tin shacks in the middle of nowhere – the villages they serve being some distance away.

The 2ft 6in gauge (762mm) line was built to convey cotton from the outlying areas to Pulgaon, where there is a massive nineteenth-century cotton factory, poignantly reminiscent of the industrial north of Victorian England. Today, this picturesque branch is paralleled throughout by a road, over which frequent buses ply their trade. Most people prefer the bus as being more reliable and make use of the train only if they are carrying heavy commodities or produce.

In the last days of steam, the line was worked by sprightly ZP class Pacifics, built by Nippon of Japan in 1954 for the Satpura lines. They were transferred to Pulgaon in 1976, and were some of the last Pacific locomotives in the world. The shortage of spare parts made maintenance a nightmare. Fortunately, only one locomotive at a time was needed in steam; the line has no crossing loops, although, in busier days, a loop did exist at Rhona Town.

On the outward journey from Pulgaon the engine ran tender first. Upon reaching Arvi the coaches were shunted round to ensure that the brake remained at the rear of the two-car train. It is said that one ton of coal was

Opposite: During its last years with steam, India's 2ft 6in (762mm) gauge Pulgaon to Arvi line was worked entirely by ZP class Pacifics, three of which had been transferred from the Satpura lines for which they were built. The ZPs were built by Nippon of Japan during the mid-1950s, but their styling was British. Here ZP No. 2 storms away from Rhona Town with train No. 644 Up, which had left Arvi at 10.40.

Above right: Indian Railways' ZP class Pacific No. 2 lifts train No. 645 Down, away from the rural station at Pachegaon. This train was the 14.30 from Pulgaon.

burnt on each trip, which seems excessive for such a small locomotive so lightly laden. However, on many rural steam-worked lines in India, coal was thrown down at strategic points along the track in return for rupees.

Punctuality on the line was the exception rather than the rule. Lateness was caused either by mechanical problems or the quality of the coal, much of which turned to clinker and clogged up the firebox, so requiring regular stops for 'blow-ups'. Another cause of delay was the engine crew's frequent tendency of stopping for prolonged tea breaks at Pargothan, irrespective of how late the train may be running.

Early in 1997, the first diesel arrived from Kurduwadi, and by June of that year steam was relegated to standby use only. Fortunately, despite the line's incredible unprofitability, Indian Railways have agreed with the British owners to continue to operate the line up to 2006.

Opposite: To the north west of Calcutta were two of McLeod & Co.'s 2ft 6in (762mm) gauge branch lines, from Burdwan and Ahmadpur that met at Katwa. Here 2-6-2 tank No. 15, built in 1930 by W.G. Bagnall of Stafford, leaves Charmardighi Halt with a Burdwan–Katwa train in January 1990.
Below: The water hydrant in the station yard at Pargothan attracts bevies of women complete with brass urns from surrounding villages. Behind, ZP class Pacific No. 2 has drawn into the platform with train No. 643 Down, which had left Pulgaon at 08.00 bound for Arvi. Trains frequently remained here for up to fifteen minutes, whether running on time or not, as the engine crew took refreshment in the local tea hut.

BRITISH MOGUL LOCOMOTIVES *Mixed traffic*

THE Mogul 2-6-0 was introduced into Britain by the Great Eastern Railway in 1878 with a class of 15 Neilson-built locomotives, the first of which carried the name *Mogul*. The most unusual Moguls to run in England were 80 locomotives imported from the US. It was very unusual for Britain, as railway builder to an empire and the world, to import locomotives, but in the late 1890s all the home builders had full order books. Known as 'Yankees', they saw service on the Midland, Great Northern and Great Central railways. They proved heavy on coal and on maintenance costs, and they had an extremely short life.

The usefulness of the Mogul as a mixed-traffic engine and for its ability to speed up freight services had been recognized. The Mogul was in effect an 0-6-0 with a leading pony truck for stability at speed. As boiler pressures became higher and superheating added to boiler efficiency, the Mogul was to become the principal British mixed-traffic engine until the 1930s, when it was augmented by 4-6-0s on heavier duties.

Amongst the most successful British Moguls was Churchward's excellent Great Western 43XX class, introduced in 1911. Other famous Moguls were Gresley's Great Northern K2s, known as 'Ragtimers', and the later Southern Railway N and U classes. Another classic

appeared in 1920 with Gresley's three-cylinder K3s. These magnificent engines performed amazing feats, running at up to 70mph (112km/h) with 600-ton freight trains. They were a dynamic forebear of Gresley's later V2 2-6-2s.

One of the last classic British Moguls was Hughes' 'Crabs' of 1926 for the London Midland & Scottish Railway. By 1932, 245 examples were in service, and they proved an excellent mixed-traffic design for the entire LMS system almost until the end of steam. When British Railways introduced its twelve standard designs for the entire country following nationalization, three Mogul classes were included.

Oppostie: The LMS Crabs were an excellent mixed-traffic Mogul. They were introduced in 1926 and, when building finished in 1932, the class totalled 245 engines. The Crabs were widely distributed around the LMS network, usually appearing on semi-fast mixed freights, but they were equally at home on medium-distance excursion trains. They were great wanderers and had a delightful tendency to turn up anywhere, often long distances from their home depot.
Above: The sylvan setting of Branston & Heighington station, which was the first south of Lincoln on the Great Northern & Great Eastern joint line to Sleaford. The train is headed by a Gresley K3 class 2-6-0 No. 61807, which was a Lincoln engine when this picture was taken on 19 May 1957.

ERITREA is Africa's newest country, born of a terrible 30-year war to gain freedom from Ethiopia. The price of independence was a ravaged country and fractured infrastructure. Its Italian-built railway, which ran 180 miles (288km) inland from the sixteenth-century Red Sea port of Massawa, through to the capital Asmara and on to Agordat near the Sudanese border, had been totally destroyed.

The track and sleepers had been ripped up for use in military bunkers all over the country, while passenger coaches were gutted to serve as sleeping quarters for soldiers.

Despite Eritrea being one of the poorest nations on earth, there is an absolute determination to rebuild the railway, and volunteer workers, some in their seventies and eighties, have come back from retirement to put the railway together again, in many cases with little more than their bare hands.

Track and sleepers have been brought back from military zones, and the line has already been laid over the 43 miles (69km) from Massawa to Ghinda.

Rolling-stock refurbishment is also well underway, with four steam locomotives in full running order. These belong to the Italian school of locomotive design and comprise two Ansaldo 0-4-4-0 four-cylinder compound Mallet tanks, along with a pair of Breda 0-4-0 well tanks, all of which date from the late 1920s. More locomotives are in the process of restoration.

Despite all odds, this unique 950mm (3ft 1³⁄₈in) gauge railway will reopen, certainly between Massawa and Asmara. Freight and passenger traffic are on the agenda, as in the longer term is tourism, as apart from the historic Mallets – which are a great attraction in themselves – the section between Asmara and Ghinda is one of the most scenic railways in the world; over the 75 miles (120km) from Massawa to Asmara, the line climbs over one mile (1.6km) in altitude, the most spectacular section being the 30 miles (48 km) between Ghinda and the capital.

The grand steaming session of Eritrea's newly restored 0-4-0 Breda well tank No. 202-004 at Asmara shed on 3 March 1998. This veteran, built as Breda No. 2272 in 1929, is seen here moving for the first time in 25 years, so representing another benchmark in the heroic revival of the steam railway in Eritrea.

Left: The return of four-cylinder compound Mallet working to Eritrea is confirmed in this scene of No. 442-59 (Ansaldo No. 1369 of 1938) seen at Digdigta, 19 miles (30km) from Massawa, whilst working out of Mai Atal with an engineers' train.
Above: The boiler of a Breda 0-4-0 well tank receives detailed attention under the sheerlegs at Asmara locomotive sheds – another benchmark in the return to life of Eritrea's steam railway.
Below: The brass worksplate of Eritrea's 0-4-4-0 Mallet four-cylinder compound, No. 442-56, built by Ansaldo as No. 1366 in 1938. With the exception of a few examples in Indonesian sugar mills, these are almost certainly the last compound Mallets in use.

AMERICAN STAPLES *Confederations and Sante Fes*

Above: A China Railway's QJ class 2-10-2 trundles across the river at Fushun with an oil train. The temperature is –23°C and the flowing swathe of the river is due to chemical discharge. Fushun's oil is produced from locally mined coal.

Opposite: South Australian Government Railways Class 520 simmers in the yard waiting for the next turn of duty. These elegant locomotives, with their light axleloading, were well suited to traversing the lightly laid tracks in the remoter areas of the state.

THE 2-10-0 never found widespread favour on America's railroads and was largely passed over in favour of the 2-10-2 Sante Fe, which rapidly established itself in the years before World War I on heavy perishable and livestock freights. Use of the Sante Fe worldwide was spasmodic, being largely absent from Britain and Europe, apart from a batch of 20 giants built by Breda and Ansaldo for Greece in 1953–4. The Sante Fe's true power-base was Russia, where some 3,220 FD class were built from 1931. These engines provided a blueprint for the China Railways later QJ 2-10-2s, some 2,500 of which remain active today.

Sante Fes appeared in Bolivia and Argentina, where they ended the steam age on the coal-carrying railway between the mines at Rio Turbio and Rio Gallegos.

The Confederations (4-8-4s) belong in the American Superpower category. It was an enlargement of the popular 4-8-2 Mountain type in an effort to obtain extra boiler and firebox capacity. The first Confederation was introduced in 1927 for the US's Northern Pacific Railroad, and the type also found favour on the Canadian National Railway. The 4-8-4 was a perfect combination with excellent riding and tracking qualities.

During the early 1930s, China received a batch of Confederations from the Vulcan Foundry in England. Classified KF1, they were designed by Colonel Kenneth Cantlie. Confederations occurred in the final steam rosters of Russia with the fabulous P36s, while Spain had an extremely handsome design, classified 242F. No Confederations survive in service.

THE DRAGONS OF SUGAR ISLAND

THE Hawaiian Philippine Company is one of Negros's largest sugar concerns and well known for its splendid Baldwin-built locomotives with huge bulbous chimneys. Officially known as 'Dragons', all engines are in radio contact with the control office, so enabling their movements throughout the 100 miles (160km) of track in the plantation to be properly co-ordinated. The company's first two Baldwin 0-6-0s were delivered in 1919, a year before the company began, and apart from a solitary 20-ton Henschel of 1923 vintage, the system is worked by larger Baldwins delivered during the 1920s. The company also has two Baldwin 0-6-2 saddle tanks, which originally worked on the company's plantations in Hawaii. These are used for shunting around the factory cane yard.

During World War II when the Japanese invasion was imminent, steps were taken to prevent the Dragons being destroyed or taken away: they were steamed up and run to the end of a mountain line where a special extension was laid to take the engines into deep undergrowth. After they had been steamed into dense vegetation, the extension track was lifted and all signs covered up. In this way, camouflaged from sight by land or air, they remained safely hidden for three years – no Japanese patrol ever located them.

All the company's engines burn bagasse, the 'free' natural waste product of the cane. Given that all mills would produce this waste fuel, it is astonishing that some mill locomotives are powered by oil. However, at the beginning of the season there is not always sufficient bagasse to go round, and certain engines at the Hawaiin Philippine Co. temporarily consume oil. This is effected by the necessary tanks being dropped into the tenders and stovepipe chimneys erected in place of the voluminous spark-arresting design.

At the start of cane cutting, it was easy to 'lose' a train on one of the many branch lines through the plantations, making photography an even greater challenge.

Above left: With the flamboyance of fairground engines on display, two of the Hawaiian-Philippine Company's Baldwin-built 'Dragons' go about their chores during the milling season. The saddle tank is an 0-6-2 of 1924, which originally came from Hawaii, whilst the larger engine is an 0-6-0 of 1920 vintage.
Above right: A hybridized and battered American Mogul of 1920s vintage, far out in the cane fields of the Ma Ao Sugar Central on the Philippine Island of Negros.
Opposite: Another scene on the metals of the Ma Ao Sugar Central on Negros, with Alco 2-6-0 No. 1 heading a night-run of empties through the plantation on the Cutcut line. This engine, in common with the ones on the previous page, is a bagasse-burner.

A LOST HERITAGE
London & North Western Railway

MANY railway historians regarded the London & North Western as the most magnificent British railway. Known as the 'Premier Line', it had the largest system, its tentacles spreading over much of England and Wales. It transformed the medieval hamlet of Crewe into a booming railway town with the most famous works in the world.

Regimented and austere in its practices, its officers were required to be gentlemen first and company servants second. The London & North Western embodied the very finest of formal British traditions.

The company's locomotive traditions were innovative, from Ramsbottom's DXs – the first standard type in the world with 947 examples being built between 1858 and 1874 – through the Webb compounds and the 4-4-0s of George Whale, to the magnificent 4-6-0s of Bowen Cooke.

As O.S. Nock so eloquently wrote, 'London & North Western engines shrieked, roared and threw fire sky-high, and were endowed with the finest set of names in locomotive history.' The LNW's engines were traditionally worked flat out, and the rhythm of cinders bouncing along the coach roofs, combined with the coach wheels over the rail joints, created a unique polyphony.

It is sad that so noble and vast a fleet of passenger locomotives should pass to extinction, with the exception of Ramsbottom's rebuilt of 2-2-2 No. 3020 *Cornwall* and Webb's 2-4-0 Jumbo No. 790 *Hardwicke* of 1892.

Amongst the classic twentieth-century designs, the last examples of the Precursor, Prince of Wales and Claughton classes were all at Crewe works for breaking up in the late 1940s, some years before the preservation movement got underway. The missing LNW legacy is by far the greatest and most serious gap in the annals of British locomotive history.

Crewe works in the summer of 1939, when the decimation of LNW types was well underway, the company having been absorbed into the LMS in 1923. In this scene are Precursor and George the Fifth 4-4-0s, Prince of Wales 4-6-0s, Coal Tanks, Bissel Trucks and Panniers. Many LNW engines were rescued from the scrap line following the outbreak of war in 1939, but following the end of hostilities, they were rapidly despatched for scrapping as the standard designs of William Stanier took over the mainstay of duties.

It is lighting-up time on a warm summer's evening as a Precursor 4-4-0 of the London & North Western Railway hurries south with a London-bound express. The carriages are painted in the LNWR colours of plum and spilt milk.

MOUNTAIN CLIMBING *Rack and pinion railways*

THERE are few railway sights more spectacular than that of a steam train ascending a mountain. Although many mountain railways are now used for tourist purposes, most were built for normal passenger services – such as the Lookout Mountain Railway in Tennessee. Rack and pinion railways developed from the realization that smooth steel locomotive wheels were unable to grip the rails on steep inclines. The world's first type of rack and pinion railway was patented as early as 1811, for use on the Middleton Colliery railway, near Leeds. Interestingly, this was not because of gradients, but because the engineer, John Blenkinsop, believed that it would be impossible for 'conventional' wheels to adhere to smooth rails at all. On the rack and pinion principle, a rack is laid between the rails and the locomotive is driven by its pinions being slotted into a geared rack.

The world's first mountain railway, designed by Sylvestre Marsh, was built in 1869 to ascend Mount Washington in New Hampshire. It was, however, the Swiss engineer Roman Abt who set the trend in Europe. One famous system on the Abt principle was the spectacular Erz, or 'Iron Mountain Railway', in Austria. This line opened in 1891 to convey iron ore from the 2,400-feet high mountain to the steel works at Donauwitz, has a maximum gradient of 1 in 14.3, over which 0-6-2 and 0-10-0 tank engines once hauled loads of up to 110 tons.

In later years, one of the world's most interesting rack and pinion sections was a stretch of 1 in 14 rack up the western side of the Heights of Lebanon on the Damascus–Beirut main line, now partly closed by war.

Above: One of the most exotic rack lines was the Sumatran coal line between Padang and Solok. E10.18, one of the 0-10-0 rank tanks built by SLM in Esslingen, Switzerland, in the 1920s is seen between Batutabal and Padang Pandjang in 1975.
Right: One of the original SLM rack tanks on the Brienz Rothorn Bahn on the shore of Lake Brienz in Switzerland. SLM is still building steam rack engines for its own rack lines and for some in other countries, such as Austria.
Opposite: The Snowdon Mountain Railway is the only rack railway in Britain, built to the Abt system in 1896. It is 4¹/₂ miles (7.2km) long.

CREATING THE COMMUTER *Suburban trains*

THE expansion of cities during the Industrial Revolution created a new pattern of urban living from about the middle of the nineteenth century. The suburban steam train, providing frequent and rapid communication to city centres, enabled commerce to become centralized within cities. In Britain and other developed areas of the world, this aspect of railway operation hastened a change in the pattern of society by providing easy and rapid travel from home to place of work.

Suburban engines were almost exclusively tank designs, as the absence of a tender made it easier to run in either direction and saved the cumbersome and time-consuming business of turning. Furthermore, the weight of water over the coupled wheels provided useful adhesion for making rapid starts from frequent stops.

The London suburbs were an obvious spawning ground, and in 1864 Beyer Peacock introduced its 4-4-0 Metropolitan tanks with 5ft 9in (175cm) driving wheels. These engines had condensing apparatus for working under the tunnels of the Metropolitan and District railways. Suburban journeys soon grew progressively longer – runs of 40 miles (64km) were not uncommon by the twentieth century. This was epitomized in Britain by the extensive networks out of London Waterloo, Victoria, Liverpool Street (with its intense 'Jazz' services) and Fenchurch Street, serving Tilbury and Southend.

Similar situations occurred in Paris, and Monet's famous paintings of Gare St Lazare caught the swirling movement of trains flitting in and out of the smoke-laden terminal. New York and Chicago had urban areas served by overhead railways, built to supplement the longer distance trains running on the main line.

The suburban steam train was the first to be replaced by electrification. The sheer density of operations adequately covered the investment, electric trains got

Opposite: A Portugese State Railway's metre gauge 0-4-4-0 Mallet
stands at the buffer stops at Oporto Trindade station late in the evening
of 12 April 1971.
Above: An Indonesian State Railway's Class C28 4-6-4 tank of superb
colonial styling seen at Tebing Tinggi, Sumatra on 7 August 1974.

CREATING THE COMMUTER

One of the world's last steam suburban services centred around Port Elizabeth and especially over the 21-mile (34km) run to Uitenhage. During the early 1970s this service was 100 per cent steam operated with North British-built Pacifics of World War I vintage. The crews had immense pride in their locomotives, and some of the trains loaded up to eleven coaches reached speeds of up to 60mph (96km/h), achieved between the frequent station stops only 2 or 3 miles apart. Pride is evident in this scene of No. 810, Class 16CR Pacific, hustling a Uitenhage-bound train near Perseverance.

away from stops more quickly than steam, and the suppression of smoke in heavily built-up areas was always an ideal. By the beginning of World War II, a considerable part of Britain's Southern railway was electrified.

Suburban steam trains have been extinct since the late 1970s. Amid the last were the 141TB and 141TC tanks working out of the Gares St Lazare and Bastille respectively. On the network of lines radiating from Buenos Aires Constitution station, the magnificent three-cylinder Vulcan Foundry-built Class 8E 2-6-4 tanks possessed the alacrity of electric traction. In Oporto, in Portugal, an antiquated array of copper-capped Victorian-style locomotives operated the dense metre gauge services out of Trindade station. This was the last magnificent flowering of a Victorian suburban system until, in the late 1970s, it, too, became a part of history.

These elegant tank locos were built by Beyer Peacock in 1913 for the State Railway Company of Holland, their principal use being for short-distance express work.

Steam suburbans survived on several lines around Paris until the early 1970s, notably with the 141TB and 141TC 2-8-2 tank classes. Here a pair of 141TCs wait to depart from the suburban station at Paris Bastille, around 1970.

HARD WORKERS FOR THE SHUNTING YARD

The severe 1 in 25 grade from Chama to Cumbres summit made it essential that freight trains were provided with banking assistance. Here Class K36 2-8-2 No. 484 banks a freight near Lobato on the Cumbres & Toltec RR; it was normal to have the caboose behind.

Above: This magnificent locomotive was the world's last banking/hump-shunting 0-8-4 tank. Built by the North British Locomotive Co. of Glasgow in 1920, it originally worked on the Great Indian Peninsular Railway as its No. 99, banking trains up the Ghats out of Bombay. It survived in industrial service at the Hindalco Aluminium smelter in Renukut until 1997, having been sold from Bombay Parel Works in 1970.
Following pages: The Lootsberg Pass in South Africa was for many years famous for its banked passenger trains. Southbound passenger trains were double-headed from Rosmead to Jagpoort from where the pilot locomotive would bank the train up the 1 in 40 grade to Lootsberg summit, leaving the train engine to continue to Graaff Reinet. Here Class 14CRB No 1882 is banked by 19D No 2692 leaving Jagpoort in May 1992.

HUMPERS and bankers form a fascinating group of engines, the sole purpose of which was slogging, brute force over short distances. Humpers were engines allocated to the large marshalling yards where hump-shunting was used. Train loads of wagons were pushed up a slope and were then, either singly or in groups, rolled by gravity down the other side to the appropriate sidings for making up train formations. This practice greatly speeded up shunting operations and was used at major marshalling yards in many parts of the world.

In Britain's hump yards, the London & North Western, North Eastern and Great Central railways all had massive tank designs of either 0-8-2 or 0-8-4 types, while in the United States, 0-8-0 tender engines were common although locomotives as large as 0-10-2s were also used.

Bankers, or 'helpers' as they were known in North America, are engines assigned to assist heavy trains over steep gradients, usually by pushing at the rear. In most cases conventional, or even relegated main line, engines would be used, but in some instances specific designs would be built. Britain's finest examples were the Midland Railway's amazing three-cylinder 0-10-0 built in 1919 for banking up the 2-mile (3.2km) Lickey Incline, with its maximum gradient of 1 in 37, and Gresley's solitary 2-8-8-2 Garratt, which spent a quarter of a century pushing coal trains up the $2^1/_2$-mile 1 in 40 Worsboro' Bank in south Yorkshire. In its later years the Garratt also had a spell on the Lickey.

The US's most celebrated helper was the Baltimore & Ohio's 0-6-6-0 four-cylinder compound No. 2400 *Old Maude*. This historic engine, which represented the Mallet's début in the US, acted as a helper on the Sand Patch grade. The Mallet also saw widespread use in US hump yards.

REDISCOVERED RELICS OF THE AZORES

The 7ft 0¹/₂in (2140mm) gauge Black Hawthorn sits on the quayside at Ponta Delgada. It was built in Gateshead as Black Hawthorn's works' number 766 in 1883 and shipped directed to the Azores.

BRUNEL'S vision of a network of 7ft 0¹/₄in (2140mm) gauge main lines was one of the most farsighted flashes of genius to emanate from nineteenth-century Britain. Were the nation – or the world – to have a network of 7ft-gauge main lines today, instead of a network of motorways, what a healthier place it would be.

Britain's broad gauge, which was confined to lines of the Great Western Railway, was abandoned in 1892, after losing the battle against the standard 4ft 8¹/₂in (1435mm) gauge pioneered by the Stephensons. The broad gauge was thenceforth regarded as extinct, with no conventional locomotive being preserved. Almost a century later, John Timson, on BBC Radio 4's Today programme, announced that two broad gauge engines had been found in the diminutive Azores Islands in the middle of the Atlantic Ocean. These islands were not known even to have a railway, and if they did it would almost certainly be an inconsequential narrow gauge line. The Azores were the very last place where one would expect to find 7ft gauge engines. The report was widely regarded as a joke, and the BBC received an incredulous response from many quarters.

But sure enough, in the harbour scrapyard at Ponta Delgada, on the island of Sao Miguel, two 7ft gauge veterans lay abandoned. Both were 0-4-0 saddle tanks, one a Black Hawthorn of Gateshead-on-Tyne dated 1883, and the other an 1888 product of the Falcon Railway Plant Works of Loughborough. They had been employed to convey boulders from an inland quarry to maintain the harbour breakwater, for as fast as the boulders were dropped into place, the ferocious Atlantic storms would wash them out to sea.

It is believed that the Azores' engines were derived from a 7ft gauge contractor's engine that had originally been used to build Brunel's broad gauge. This had been subsequently sold to the harbour authorities in Holyhead to maintain their breakwater. In later years, this engine was transferred from Holyhead to the Azores for similar work, so establishing the gauge there, and subsequent engines built new for the Azores followed suit. The two Ponta Delgada engines are the only 'genuine' broad gauge locomotives in the world.

Top left: The worksplate carried by the Falcon 0-4-0 saddle tank reveals her date of manufacture to have been 1888.

Top right: The precedent for a broad gauge system was set by Isambard Kingdom Brunel, and this down express is passing Stoke Canon Junction on the English Great Western Railway. A point of interest is the slotted post with its spectacle frame and lamp. Note the lighting and maintenance platform just below the lamp.

Above: The world's last two broad gauge locomotives sit within feet of one another, and here the Black Hawthorn (left) measures up to the Falcon, built by Hughes Henry & Co. at Falcon Works in Loughborough in 1888. The following year Falcon was acquired by the British Electric Light Corporation and the new company became British Electrical Engineering Co., which survives today as one of Britain's few locomotive builders.

Left: Despite the decline of steam workings around the world, building still continues, albeit spasmodically, at Tangshan works in China. This scene was taken on New Year's Day 1992 in the erecting shop at Tangshan showing newly assembled SY class 2-8-2 industrial Mikado No.1722.

Above: A welder fabricates detailed parts for locomotives at Tangshan works.

TANGSHAN will probably go down in history for building the world's last steam locomotives; these were still being produced, albeit on a vastly reduced scale, in the early months of 1998. In 1976, Tangshan was in the world news following a disastrous earthquake, measuring 7.8 on the Richter Scale, which reduced the city to ruins, with a staggering death toll of 242,000 from a population of 1.06 million. The city was virtually wiped from the face of the earth, and Tangshan was compared with Pompeii.

Today a new city has risen from the ashes of that vile night and the locomotive works are one of many thriving enterprises. Its exclusive production is the SY class – a classic American-styled light Mikado – of which some 1,800 are in service throughout China. Tangshan also exports locomotives, notably a batch of French-idiom metre gauge SY2s for North Vietnam in 1965.

In November 1987, *Railway Gazette International* announced that Tangshan was launching an export drive for its SYs. Sadly, there was little response, although the Valley Railway Corporation in the US did order one locomotive for hauling tourist excursions. Another was ordered for the New York Susquehanna Railway in Weston, but this locomotive was lost at sea, having had to be dumped overboard during a violent storm in transit.

During the late 1980s a small number of SYs was built at the Tongling locomotive works and other works may have also produced the class. The SYs have permeated Chinese industry and ousted virtually all other classes. Many will remain into the next century. With steam becoming increasingly threatened on China's main lines, the honours may well fall on the SY to be the world's last steam locomotive type in commercial service.

JAVAN SUGAR FIELDS

Above: A typical rural scene out in the plantations which serve the Trangkil sugar mill at Pati, Java, showing the improvised field track dropped in place to bring the loaded cane wagons up to the 'main line'. The engine in the background is the mill's famous No. 4, Britain's last steam locomotive export, built by Hunslet of Leeds in 1971.
Left: Close up details of No. 4's worksplate.

Opposite: An afternoon session at Karanglegi Lor on the Trangkil sugar system in Java reveals Hunslet 0-4-2 saddle tank No. 4 waiting for the wagons to be loaded with cane. This humble tank engine was the last of the tens of thousands of locomotives which rolled from British foundries to take the Industrial Revolution to all corners of the earth.

OVER the last 30 years of steam operation, Java has held a unique position. It first achieved fame in the 1960s, when it was discovered that Java and Sumatra had a vast array of antiquated locomotives covering a variety of gauges. The extent of the treasures that Java held on its main line railways were revealed in A.E. Durrant's erudite book *PNKA Power Parade*, published in 1974. This detailed engines ranging from huge metre gauge 2-8-8-0 Mallets and Sharp Stewart 2-4-0 passenger engines of the 1870s to 0-4-0 Beyer Peacock tram engines as depicted on page 142, along with standard gauge Beyer Peacock 0-6-0s.

No sooner had this treasure house been discovered than it began to disappear. Indonesia's booming economy transformed the country; within ten years some main line railways were closed and the remainder was modernized.

But this was only half the story, for Java is a major sugar producer; the numerous mills were almost all rail-connected and used an incredible variety of European industrials from such builders as Ducroo & Braun of Holland and Orenstein & Koppel of Germany. Every mill seemed to have a different type of locomotive and certainly a different colour scheme. During the last years of main line operation, the plantation railways had been largely overlooked. But as one of the world's major steam enclaves, Java is as important to European industrial steam as Cuba is to American locomotive traditions.

During the 1997 milling season over 100 locomotives were at work embracing at least five gauges, ranging from 600mm to 750mm (1ft 11½in to 2ft 5½in). Many engines are hybridized, battered, multi-hued relics, others are maintained in a workmanlike condition.

The vast majority are bagasse-burners, so providing free fuel without dependence on oil. Bagasse is low in calorific value so enormous quantities are required to maintain steam, especially when working heavy trains. At night the effects are spectacular as the engines emit shrouds of flaming bagasse into the night skies.

Many of the engines are confined to shunting operations around the mills, but others work out into the cane fields serving remote loading sidings to which cane is delivered by bullock-cart, tractor or lorry. The island holds the world's last enclave of Mallets and also the world's last jackshaft-driven engine, in the form of a yellow-liveried 0-8-0 tender tank, built by Orenstein & Koppel in 1910 and named *Salak* after an extinct volcano. Said to be the most powerful engine in Java, its geared drive ensures sure-footedness on wet rails.

There is every hope that at least some of the veterans will see service into the twenty-first century, by which time Java will have reverted to its position of 30 years ago, in holding the world's oldest and most varied steam survivors.

Orenstein & Koppel's 0-8-0 tank Klein Linder No.11 *Guntur* hard at work on the 700mm (2ft 3½in) gauge network at the Purwodadi sugar mill in Madiun, Java. The engine is seen alongside a bullock-cart, which is delivering cane to the railhead ready to be transferred to the factory by train.

This delightful engine was built by Borsig of Berlin in 1912 as an 0-8-0 tank with Klein Linder axles. She was formally named *Garuda* and is running here as a tender tank. The engine was built during Borsig's 'English Phase', during which many of their locomotives were designed with a distinct British appearance. The sandman's job is to ride on the front of the locomotive and manually spray the track with sand to prevent slipping when working over tracks made wet and muddy by the frequent tropical storms which occur during the milling season.

THE 10-WHEELER OF AMERICAN FOLKLORE

Above: Pennsylvania Railroad No. 20 was one of the famous G-5f class, known as the 'Pittsburgh Commuter Engine'. Built at Altoona, the class totalled 121 examples, 90 for the Pennsylvania Railroad, built between 1923 and 1925, and 31 for the Long Island Railroad, between 1924 and 1929. With 69-inch (175cm) drivers, they showed a superb turn of speed and were able to get heavy trains on the move in record time.
Opposite: This sprightly 10-wheeler worked the 150-mile (240km) copper-hauling Nevada Northern Railroad. Built by Baldwin in 1910, it was was caught complete with wooden baggage car at East Ely, Nevada.

THE 10-wheeler, America's second most popular type, lay at the heart of American railroad folklore, especially with the high-drivered variety, which was responsible for so many fast passenger trains. It was beautifully epitomized by Meade Lux Lewis's epic boogie piece 'Six-Wheeled Chaser', which elegantly portrays the rhythms of a fast passenger train, when the type was pre-eminent in this form of service.

Following the celebrated reign of the 4-4-0, the 10-wheeler became popular by the 1870s, and powerful, big-boilered examples with 54in (137cm) diameter drivers were hauling passenger trains through the Rocky Mountains during the 1880s. Its golden years were between 1870 and the end of the century, when it was partly replaced by the Atlantic with its wide firebox potential. Virtually all railroads had 10-wheelers whose ultimate fate on fast passenger work was sealed by the all-pervading Pacific, which combined the advantages of both 4-6-0 and the Atlantic.

Ten-wheelers, however, retained a leading role in many rosters until 1910, and never entirely disappeared on secondary freight, commuter and branch line duties. The Pennsylvania G class of the 1920s was the last 4-6-0 to be built for commuter service (4-6-0s were never a common choice for such trains) on non-electrified lines.

The 10-wheeler, like the 4-4-0 before it, symbolized the age when railways were paramount, before the encroachment of road traffic. The wide diversity of uses on which the type appeared throughout some three-quarters of a century in the US was reflected in export packages. Classic American 10-wheelers saw service in many countries of the world, on a wide variety of gauges, where many survived until the end of steam. Some classic American 10-wheelers survive in South America.

SUNLIGHT, SMOKE AND SHADOW
Inside a large locomotive depot

FEW people could fail to be thrilled by the atmosphere of a large steam locomotive depot, where intense concentrations of roaring and hissing locomotives exude a feeling of enormous power. The busy steam depot is a place of feverish activity, with locomotives going through the labour-intensive operations of being coaled, watered, having their fires raked on the ash pits, oiled and turned. Those engines that are dead, having boiler washouts or repairs, form an exciting backdrop to the perpetual motion of locomotives coming on and going off shed.

It is these multifarious activities, combined with the vibrant, pulsating locomotives that make the depots so thrilling. Many large sheds had round-the-clock shifts known as 'yard arrangers' whose job it was to ensure that each locomotive was properly attended to according to its needs, and on the right line, in the right place, fully prepared to leave on time.

These great concentrations of steam conjure up the very essence of the industrial smoke-stack revolution – mystical potions of smoke and steam emanating from the locomotives merging with the sunlight streaming through blackened windows. A busy steam shed conveys the sense of atmosphere that imbues Monet's series of paintings at Gare St Lazare in Paris and, although such effects were commonplace in depots around the world, there are now only a handful of locations left on earth that recall this industrial drama of a bygone age. It lingers yet at Bulawayo in Zimbabwe where 15 Garratts remain active.

A Dutch Rhenish Railway 4-4-0, introduced in 1889 lurks in the gloom between duties. Nicknamed 'Rhine Bogies', they handled Dutch expresses until superseded by more powerful locomotives.

A scene in the busy motive power depot at Anshan Iron & Steelworks in China. Anshan is China's iron and steel capital, and the entire complex employs some 40 locomotives on internal duties. The engines are serviced at this busy running shed set within the complex. The example seen here is a standard SY industrial Mikado.

Sunlight, smoke and shadow

Above: Another scene inside the locomotive sheds in Anshan Iron & Steel Works featuring two industrial Class SY Mikados. Although Anshan Works employs a number of different classes, these SYs are the predominant type. Opposite: A vibrant scene at the once busy locomotive sheds at Harbin in north-eastern China. Harbin is an important junction and once had an allocation of over 100 engines which served a number of different routes, in particular the busy main line south though Manchuria. This scene is taken in the watering, sanding and fire-raking bays.

ECHOES OF THE RAJ 1903

WHAT was once good for Britain was good for the rest of the world too. The railways of most lands under British rule echoed those of the mother country, and India's were no exception.

Building the railways of the Indian subcontinent was one of Britain's greatest historical achievements. The system was built in all its diversity by companies based in London, by organizations under Indian Government control or by the rulers of the various states. As the network grew towards the end of the nineteenth century, a great diversity of locomotive types was being ordered from British manufacturers.

In response to calls for greater economy, and a military preference for standard types that could be moved about more easily in the event of war, it was decided to produce a number of basic designs that would operate as standard types throughout the subcontinent. To meet this call, the British Engineering Standards Association (BESA) was formed and involved some pre-eminent British locomotive engineers.

For India's standard gauge lines two predictable types were chosen initially – an inside-cylinder 0-6-0 and an inside-cylinder 4-4-0, the two types having a common boiler. These were followed by an Atlantic and a 4-6-0 – the relative merits of the two types being a current debate at home. For heavy freight a 2-8-0 was chosen.

The shape, size and form of these engines were a mirror image of development in Britain. Some of the BESA standards were built in large numbers and influenced the shape of Indian steam for over half of the twentieth century. The 4-6-0 was particularly successful and examples, in modified form, continued to be supplied to India until as late as 1950. Variations took account of such developments as superheating.

Pakistan Railways SGS class inside-cylindered 0-6-0 No. 2477 storms through a rocky defile with the 1400 Khewra–Dandot on 21 January 1977. This service was a 'mixed' train, carrying freight and passenger traffic, and included a through coach from Lahore.

Top: The last survivor of Indian Railways' HSM class 2-8-0s, No. 26190, at Fort Gloster on the River Hoogley, having worked a pick-up freight. Built by Armstrong Whitworth in 1924, this last survivor of these former Bengal & Nagpur locomotives was allocated to Santragachi sheds in Calcutta.

Above: A builder's study of one of Robinson's Atlantics for the Great Central Railway. They were similar to the magnificent BESA Atlantics that formed part of the Indian Railways' locomotive standard series.

ECHOES OF THE RAJ 1920s

Above: One of the last surviving Indian Railways' XD class 2-8-2s, No. 22372, is seen working from Dornakal Junction shed and is caught on line with coal empties bound for nearby thermal power stations between Karapelli Junction and Bhadhrachalan Road. It was built by the North British Locomotive Co. of Glasgow in 1946.
Opposite: One of the last Indian Railways' standard XE Mikados to receive a major overhaul at Jamalpur works was No. 22542, built by the legendary Clydeside shipbuilder Beardmore of Dalmuir in 1930. The engine returned to its home depot at Asansol on the eastern coalfield of Bengal on 12 December 1976 and is caught here on running-in duties around the shed yard.

AS the railways of the Indian subcontinent developed, an inevitable need arose for greater power than the BESA designs could produce. The narrow firebox of these engines was not well suited to the poor quality coal available, and in 1924 a Locomotive Standards Committee was formed to devise a new set of 'national standards'.

On the broad gauge (5ft 6in/1676mm), three classes of Pacific and two classes of Mikado were conceived. These became the famous 'X' series of the late 1920s. The Pacifics were comprised of XA (light), XB (medium fast and mail trains) and XC (heavy long distance). For freight, the XD Mikado (medium hauls) and the massive XE (heavy mineral). These exciting engines represented a massive increase in power and were all equipped with wide fireboxes to cope with inferior coal.

The Xs were superb aesthetically, and in common with their BESA counterparts represented the latest state of development in the mother country. Pacifics and Mikados were being introduced in Britain at the same time as the Xs were being designed. The XC and XE bore a striking resemblance to Gresley's A3s and P1s respectively, although the Indian engines had two cylinders as opposed to three on Gresley's designs.

Inevitably many non-standard types were also supplied, including some four-cylinder Pacifics and the massive Garratts supplied to the Bengal Nagpur Railway.

The metre gauge (3ft 3³/₈in), which represented a large part of the Indian railway system, also had a set of standards. Known as the Ys, these consisted of YB and YC Pacifics and YD Mikados. Standard designs were also prepared for the 2ft 6in (762mm) gauge lines. Known as the Zs, these included Prairies, Mikados and Pacifics – all designs with sufficient flexibility to cope with the often indifferent tracks of secondary, usually rural systems.

The 1920s' Standards remained in evidence almost until the end of steam, albeit in ever-dwindling numbers, gradually ousted by the post-war generation of engines.

Few nations have ever attempted to embark on such a cohesive standardization programme. The fascinating paradox is that India, in all her cultural and geographical diversity, ended up with one of the most multifarious fleets of locomotives the world has ever seen to the delight of the railway historian and doubtless many Indians too.

Above: The last surviving Indian Railways XB class Pacific was No. 22153 allocated to Rajamundry. It had been built by the Vulcan Foundry, Lancashire, in 1927, for the Madras & Southern Mahratta Railway. The XBs were an important class of express and mail engine and were widely used throughout the Indian subcontinent. It was caught here on 13 November 1979 leaving Rajamundry shed to take the 20.35 passenger train to Bhimavaran.

Indian Railway's last surviving XC class Pacific was No. 22224, a Vulcan Foundry engine of 1929, originally built for the East Indian Railway. It was allocated to Burdwan depot in Bengal and ended its days working the daily pick-up freight to Bolpur, where it was caught drifting though the cutting at Prantik on 8 March 1981.

STANDARD DESIGNS OF POST-WAR INDIA

DURING World War II India received a range of austerity designs that were wholly American inspired. The war vastly increased traffic throughout the subcontinent, and an incredible 909 5ft 6in (1676mm) gauge freight locomotives were brought into service from American and Canadian builders. They comprised United States Army Transportation Corps S160 2-8-0s, classified AWC, some huge Mikados classified AWE, which were American austerity versions of the British XE, and the general-purpose light Mikado classified AWD/CWD.

The rugged utilitarian nature of the American engines proved popular in India, and following the war virtually all new locomotives supplied to the subcontinent were of American derivation. After the war and before independence, Baldwin had consultations with India Railways and produced the first of a new series of Pacifics classified WP. These were semi-streamlined and proved ideal for working India's heavy long-distance expresses, which needed to be kept rolling at speeds of 40–50 mph (64–80km/h). The engines were free-steaming, robust and trouble-free and the class had reached a total of 755 engines when building finished in 1967. The WPs were built in Canada, Austria, Poland and India – a very different situation from Britain's virtual monopoly of the previous hundred years.

Even more significant was the WG Mikado, which had the same boiler, motion and other parts as the WP. The first hundred of these were built in Britain in 1950, but the majority of the eventual total of 2,450 examples were built at India's Chittaranjan works.

Inevitably the steam age was brought to a close on 5ft 6in gauge metals with WPs and WGs, along with a handful of the lighter Class WL Pacifics. The country's last metre gauge main line operations will cease by the year 2000. The final scenes are now being played out by American-inspired YP Pacifics and YG Mikados, both of which date from the post-war period, the class totals for these engines being 871 and 1,074 examples respectively.

Left: One of the last survivors of India's once numerous WG class 2-8-2 Mikados was No. 9428, a Canadian Locomotive Works engine of 1956. No. 9428 was pensioned off to the cement factory at Chunar for a further lease of active life and is seen here at the stabling point with the cement factory in the background on 5 January 1997.

Opposite: Elaborate decorations were often applied to a steam locomotive in India when it hauled a special train. This WP Pacific No. 7715 had been embellished for the Minister of Railways when it was photographed on a Daund–Manmad passenger working at Visapur in November 1987.

THE ROMANCE OF THE NIGHT TRAIN

AS part of the celebrations of World Book Day on 23 April 1998, the two children of British Prime Minister Tony Blair each chose their favourite poem for him to read to a meeting of 200 children at the sixteenth-century Globe Theatre in South London. His young son, Euan, 14, choose W.H. Auden's 'Night Mail', which celebrates the sheer magic of the railway at night. The poem was written at a time when the railway was the nation's heartbeat – the pulse and pace of society, industry and commerce.

The role of the railway as a nation's principal form of transport inevitably meant working around the clock (and still does for freight and the few remaining sleeper trains). During the great age of railways, the industry never slept: freight, passenger and mail trains rolled through the night with traffic sometimes little diminished from that of the daylight hours.

The noises of the vast marshalling yards resounded though the night, as the endless process of splitting freight trains and remarshalling the wagons into formations for the next section of their journey was carried out at all important junctions.

The distant sound of engines shunting through the night was a lovely aspect of the steam age. On clear nights, especially after rain, the sounds would become crystal clear, carrying over several miles. The hollow rasps of the locomotive's exhaust, the roar of slipping wheels when moving a heavy load, the piping whistle calls, the rushes of steam and the musical clank of wagons evoked an almost mystical presence, a symphony of sound which, in its endless variety, engendered slumber and evoked feelings of security – all was well with the world.

The magic of the steam train is understood and appreciated by millions of people the world over; nowhere was that magic better epitomized than under the veil of darkness, which enabled the glorious sights and sounds to stand out to maximum effect.

Sugar-cane milling on Java is an around-the-clock activity during the intensity of the campaign, which lasts over several months. Here, at Pagottan mill, No. 7, an 0-10-0 tender tank with Luttermöller axles, built by Orenstein & Koppel in 1926, heads a rake of cane to the factory.

Victorian Railway Class S 4-6-2 No. 1928, one of four streamlined
locomotives, sits under the yard lights on a warm Australian
night. Intended for the prestigious 'Spirit of Progress' express, the class
earned a reputation for speed and efficiency.

Above: A night freight leaves Olavarria to head out across the lonely Argentine pampas, headed by a former Buenos Aires & Great Southern Railway 5ft 6in (1676mm) gauge 11B class 2-8-0 of which 100 were built.
Opposite: This delightful engine, decked in a riot of highly saturated hues, in accordance with traditional Hindu art, was caught at Lucknow. It is one of Indian Railway's 5ft 6in (1676mm) gauge XT class 0-4-2 tanks, which consisted of 77 engines, most of which were built in Germany by Krupp at Essen between 1929 and 1936, with later engines coming from India's Ajmer works during the late 1940s.

STEAM IN THE SNOW

THE animated sight of steam trains set amid the great landscapes of the world has long been an enduring theme for photographs. And if that landscape is covered in snow, so much the better, for like a wolf howling on the Siberian taiga, or an elephant trumpeting its way through the African Bush, the beauty of a steam train shrieking its way across a snowy terrain is a never-to-be-forgotten experience (why else the long railway scenes in David Lean's *Doctor Zhivago*?).

There are but half a dozen places left on earth where such sights can be found. Gone are the days of steam on the Canadian Pacific, where several engines and a snow plough would be engaged in clearing one stretch of line. Gone too, are the days when American-inspired Finnish wood-burners crossed the Arctic Circle and proceeded through blizzards into snowbound Lapland. No more do giant Russian engines steam across the wintry vastness of Siberia.

Today, the best of the magic is to be found in China, and the small town of Nancha is one of the exotic places which springs to mind. Nancha is a junction town and the route northwards to Yichun involves a steep gradient out of the town, necessitating a banker over the 2-mile (3.2km) stretch to the summit. Southbound trains also climb with a banker for 2 miles from the country station of Luisha to the summit before dropping down into Nancha. Winter temperatures at Nancha can fall to −35°C, and it may require several hours at the summit to photograph three or four trains. But, in spite of the feasome cold and hours of waiting, the dramas which ensue are worth every second.

Above: Whatever the situation, the steam locomotive always seemed to fit well into the landscape. On a clear, moonlit night with a fresh fall of snow, a London Midland & Scottish Railway Duchess 4-6-2 heads a northbound express through the fells.

Opposite: A geared Heisler locomotive trundles over the metals of the Chesapeake & Ohio en route from a lumber company in West Virginia to the Cass Scenic Railway in December 1966. The Heisler, Shay and Climax represent the three most common types of geared steam locomotive. Slow but powerful, these geared engines were capable of hauling over grades as steep as 1 in 12.5.

Above: A Finnish Railway's TR1 class 2-8-2 No. 1074 near Rovaniemi on the Arctic Circle. The engine has just returned from Lapland, having left Rovaniemi at 02.41 to collect gravel and return laden to Rovaniemi.

Opposite: A China Railway's QJ Class 2-10-2 vigorously attacks Nancha Bank with a freight train bound for Yichun. The engine's exhaust rises ever-higher into the clear blue sky and seemingly never evaporates in temperatures which can reach as low as −35°C. Nancha is distinctive in being one of last stretches of main line railway anywhere in the world on which steam banking engines are regularly employed.

CHINESE DRAGONS

DURING the 1990s China has become the last country in the world where steam still performs a significant role on the national railway system, with more active steam locomotives than the rest of the world combined. As recently as 1988, China had 11,000 active 'Dragons'. Up to 1990, India rivalled China as a steam country, but it chose to discard steam in a precipitate and wasteful manner.

Until the late 1970s, it was almost impossible to visit China, and tales of what might exist there were rampant. Would it be possible to find American 4-4-2 tanks from Brooks Locomotive Works in New Jersey, Japanese-built streamlined Pacifics from the South Manchurian Railway or ex-Great Western Dean Goods 0-6-0s?

Sadly for those with such hopes, the fall of the Bamboo Curtain revealed a very different kind of railway

– one that was modern and highly standardized. Thirty years of Communist rule had allowed China's railway to flourish. Much of the system had to be rebuilt following the war with Japan and civil war. Once the Communists assumed control in 1949, they rebuilt the damaged sections and constructed many new lines. Of the 11,000 steam locomotives in 1988, over 10,000 were accounted for by six principal classes – QJ 2-10-2s; JS and JF 2-8-2s; the SL6 and RM Pacifics plus the SY industrial Mikado.

What China lacked in variety, it made up for in quality, for nowhere else on earth could huge steam locomotives be seen being put through their paces on busy main lines with trains of enormous weight. These dramas were set amid some of the world's most exciting scenery and climatic diversity. China represents steam's last fling.

Opposite left:
This delightfully
embellished SY
class 2-8-2 was
caught working at
Tangshan colliery.
Opposite right:
A brand new QJ
class 2-10-2 peeps
out from the
gloomy depths of
the steam testing
shed at Datong
Locomotive Works.
Left: The pride of
Harbin was QJ class
2-10-2 No. 2470
Zhou De. Very few
steam locomotives
in China carried
names, but the few
that did were
lavishly embellished.
In this case, the
engine carried a
brass cast of Zhou
De, who was one
of Mao's generals in
the revolution.

MIKADOS *A great British export*

THE Mikado was one of the most prevalent locomotive types, yet, curiously, it was all but absent from Britain's indigenous list. It did, however, occur prolifically in British export orders in the first half of the twentieth century with a wide variety of designs for various gauges.

In Britain it was adopted only by Gresley on the London & North Eastern Railway. He introduced it in 1925 with his magnificent P1s, which were principally employed on heavy mineral drags between Peterborough and Ferme Park (London), over which they were capable of taking 100-wagon trains of 1,600 tons in weight. The P1s were generic to Gresley's famous Pacifics, the two types having a common boiler. Awesome though the P1s were, they were eclipsed by the even more spectacular P2s, introduced in 1934 for the heavily graded section between Edinburgh and Aberdeen.

The P1 class comprised only two engines, and only six P2s were built. Both the P1s were withdrawn in July 1945, immediately after the war, while the P2s were rebuilt into Pacifics by Gresley's successor Edward Thompson. These eight locomotives were destined to represent the Mikado in Britain, the mother country of railways.

Serious consideration was given to a two-cylinder Mikado for heavy freight when the standard designs of the newly nationalized British Railways were being prepared in the late 1940s and early 1950s. By that time, engines with wide fireboxes were considered necessary because good quality coal was becoming more expensive and less abundant. In the event, the wide firebox 2-10-0 was chosen following experience with the Austerity 2-10-0s produced during the war. This was clearly the right choice as the 9Fs – as the new engines were known – proved to be one of the most successful types in British locomotive history.

Opposite: The most spectacular of all exported British Mikados were the XEs for India. Introduced in 1928 in the mould of the P1s, they were the most powerful conventional engines to work on the Indian subcontinent. The last survivor is seen here in January 1997, ending its days on coal hauls from Manikpur Colliery to Korba thermal power station in Madhya Pradesh. This superb engine was the sole surviving engine built by the legendary Clydeside shipbuilder Beardmore of Dalmuir.

Above: This 1930s scene gives an idea of the magnificence of Gresley's later P2 Mikado, showing the P2's 6ft 2in (188cm) diameter driving wheels for fast mixed-traffic work compared with the P1's 5ft 2in (157cm) wheels.

Left: A Gresley P1, which from the front is almost indistinguishable from his A1 Pacifics. Similarly, India's XE Mikados and XC Pacifics also bore a striking similarity to each other. All were clearly influenced by Gresley.

THE STREAMLINED AGE

Above: The sleek streamlined form of China Railways SL7 class Pacific No. 751. Introduced during the 1930s, these engines were streamlined in accordance with contemporary world practice. Their design was similar to the New York Central's K5 Pacifics that worked the 'Mercury Express'.

Opposite: Streamlining for greater efficiency ranged from the graceful lines of such locomotives as the New York Central's Class J-3a to the derisory attempts of England's Great Western Railway. One of the most striking European efforts was the Belgian National Railway Class 12 4-4-2 seen here.

THE Art Deco period of the 1930s embraced all aspects of society: architecture, interior design, jewellery, utensils and clothes. Railway companies around the world readily embraced the idea of streamlined trains because air-smoothed casings were seen as an excellent way of drawing attention back to railways, which were beginning to be upstaged by planes and automobiles encroaching on their monopoly.

The first streamlined steam locomotive in the US was the New York Central's magnificent streamlined Hudson, *Commodore Vanderbilt*, built in 1934 for working between New York and Chicago. This striking locomotive was conceived after wind-tunnel tests. The New York Central also had their astonishing J3 Hudsons, which had streamlining designed by Henry Dreyfuss, for working the 'Twentieth Century Limited'.

As the fashion took hold, many striking shapes appeared on other railroads. Many of them, however, were little more than shrouds applied to existing engines, providing no actual benefit in performance, and in many cases the casings were short-lived.

In 1934 the German Reichsbahn applied partial covering to one of their three-cylinder Class 03 Pacifics, which was followed up in 1935–7 by three fabulous three-cylinder 4-6-4s with 7ft 6½in (230cm) diameter driving wheels. Classified 05, these striking locomotives easily reached speeds of 110 mph (176km/h), and a speed of 124 mph (198km/h) was claimed for one at the head of a 194-ton train.

The spirit was fully captured in Britain by the London Midland & Scottish and London & North Eastern railways as they vied for supremacy of various kinds over the West and East Coast main lines respectively, with Stanier's Princess Coronations on the former and Gresley's A4s on the latter.

Perhaps the most astonishing streamlined locomotive of all was the Pennsylvanian 4-4-4-6 of 1939, which was exhibited at the New York World Fair as the biggest express locomotive in the world. This locomotive had its casing designed by Raymond Loewy.

Changing fashions, and the advent of World War II, spelt the end of streamlined trains around the world. Perhaps the most dramatic exception was Gresley's LNER A4s that retained their casing until they were replaced by diesels in the 1960s, although the valances and other fine details, removed during the war, were never replaced.

Partial streamlining remained with India's WP Pacifics, which survived in service until the 1990s, and Bulleid's West Country and Battle of Britain classes, some of which ran in their air-smoothed condition until final withdrawal in 1967.

Above: The first of William Stanier's superb Princess Coronation class streamlined Pacifics No. 6220
Coronation stands at Euston as a new engine in 1938. Princess Coronations worked the West Coast main
line between London Euston and Glasgow. By 1949 those members of the class which had
been streamlined had all lost their casings, unlike their rivals, the Gresley A4s on the East Coast main line,
which retained their casings until withdrawal from service.
Opposite: The sleek streamlined form of China Railway's SL7 Pacific No. 751. These engines once
worked the high-speed luxury air-conditioned 'Asia Express' between Dalian – then known as
Port Arthur – on the Yellow Sea coast, and Shenyang – known as Mukden – and Harbin during the
Japanese occupation of Manchuria.

WORKING THE COALFIELDS OF ASSAM

FROM the early East India Company trading base of Calcutta, the British sailed north in Scottish-built paddle steamers; they plied their way up the rivers of what is now Bangladesh to enter the mighty Brahmaputra River and sail due eastwards into the dense, inhospitable, leech-ridden jungles of Assam. All of north-east India became part of the Bengal Presidency of British India in 1838, and steps were taken to develop the region and generate agricultural and commercial revenues.

Intrepid pioneers were offered incentives to set up plantations of rubber, hemp, jute and – most importantly – tea. They also created thriving mineral industries, opening up coal, limestone and iron mines, and it was perhaps inevitable that some form of British industrial locomotive should follow to serve their enterprises.

The Assam Railways & Trading Co. was founded in 1881, and the first Bagnall arrived on the coalfield in 1894. Between then and 1931, fifteen Stafford-built locomotives were delivered to a standard 2 ft (610mm) gauge Bagnall design. Operating conditions in this industrial outpost are rough. Maintaining the Bagnalls over recent decades has not been easy, and the fleet has been supplemented by four of Sharp Stewart's celebrated B class 0-4-0s from the Darjeeling Himalayan Railway.

To serve the collieries, a brickworks, complete with a Manchester kiln, was built at Ledo, and to this day, gangs of gaily dressed women hack the clay from the earth and, having loaded it into wicker baskets, manually fill the diminutive wagons of the waiting train. After several hours, the train begins its precarious journey over the rickety weed-strewn tracks to the brickworks.

The Assam coalfields evoke a feeling reminiscent of earlier industrial times in Britain; they are a place where time has stood still for over a century. Collieries and slag tips coexist with the workers' tiny dwellings, around which ragged children play and animals abound. The valleys are shrouded in a smoky haze caused by the open coal fires of the dwellings and, silhouetted against the hills, are the smoking boiler-house chimneys of those collieries that raise the coal by steam, while locomotive sounds, day and night, give piquancy to an incomparable industrial landscape.

Above: A standard 2ft (610mm) gauge Bagnall 0-4-0 saddle tank, built as the company's works' number 1556 of 1899, trundles a trainload of clay towards Ledo Brickworks on the Margherita Mine's complex on the Upper Assam coalfield.
Above right: Bagnall 0-4-0 saddle tank *David*, built as the company's

No. 2132 of 1924, heads a train of loaded coal tubs from the underground mine at Tirap.
Opposite: Bagnall 0-4-0 saddle tank No. 1733 of 1904 *Ram Ring* brings a trainload of coal up to the Lancashire boiler house on the Namdang Colliery network of Upper Assam.

THE MOUNTAINS *Built for power*

THE American Mountain type – the 4-8-2 – first appeared in the US on the Chesapeake & Ohio Railway in 1911 for hauling heavy passenger trains through West Virginian mountain country. The Mountain type provided an increase in power over the Mikado, and the four-wheeled bogie gave better tracking characteristics for fast running.

Various other US lines followed until the 4-8-2 supplemented the Pacific for operating the heaviest passenger trains on steeply graded sections. The Mountains offered speed and power, and in the years following World War I, the type appeared on many of the heaviest and fastest freight trains in the US and Canada.

However, these were not the world's first Mountains; that distinction goes to South Africa, where six 1904-built 4-8-0s for the Natal Government Railways were fitted with a trailing bissel truck in 1906 to make them the world's first 4-8-2s. The first of a class of new Mountains arrived from Glasgow in 1909.

From then on, the 4-8-2 became a prominent type on the newly formed South African Railways, eventually numbering over 1,400 locomotives. They provided the power, flexibility and relatively light axleloading necessary for the difficult conditions on the 3ft 6in (1067mm) gauge network. For similar reasons, Mountains also saw use in many other parts of Africa. The introduction of the Class 15CB 4-8-2s from Baldwin in 1925 led to a weakening of British design influence in favour of American practice.

Mountains were almost absent from Britain and many European countries, most noticeably Russia, though France, Spain and Czechoslovakia all had examples. Spain was a particularly important user over the later years of steam development and had some magnificent streamlined examples, which superficially resembled Gresley's A4s in Britain. Mountains never occurred on the main lines of the Indian subcontinent or Japan and only in a very limited form in China. The latter days of steam development in New Zealand saw some powerful 4-8-2s introduced in 1939.

In Latin America, Bolivia and Chile both had a roster of Mountain types, as did Argentina on the metre gauge (3ft 3⅜in) Belgrano Railway.

A busy scene in May 1992 at the recently dieselized Rustenberg Platinum Mines in the Transvaal as a double-headed pair of Class 15F 4-8-2s arrive on a loaded ore train while a sister 15F takes water on the left.

BRITISH CLASSICS OF URUGUAY

Mixed freight to Fray Bentos. This scene in Uruguay depicts the sole remaining T class 2-8-0 No. 139 *Ing Pedro Magnou* at the head of a mixed freight. Note the position of the nameplate on the side of the engine's firebox. Named after a famous Uruguayan engineer, this superb locomotive has a distinct Highland Railway aura and is the kind of engine one might have found working in the Scottish Highlands during the 1920s.

BRITISH interests in the building and operating of Uruguay's railways were extensive, and this is eloquently reflected in the locomotive heritage. It mirrored that of the mother country; add the names of the pre-nationalization companies – Central, Midland, North Western and Northern – and the reflection is almost complete. Walk beneath the portals of Montevideo's Central Articas station and you might be at London St Pancras.

Uruguay's latter-day steam roster was comprised primarily of Moguls and 2-8-0s. The former came from Beyer Peacock in Manchester, the latter from Hawthorn Leslie in Newcastle-on-Tyne.

On a visit to the locomotive sheds at Paysandu in 1980, 19 engines were present, all from Beyer Peacock's works. The oldest was a 2-6-0 tank of the 1880s and the most recent a pair of Z class Moguls exported in 1929. These were particularly interesting in having a British London & North Western Railway-style smokebox door.

Magnificent as the above classes were, they were eclipsed by the three surviving 4-4-4 suburban tanks built by the Vulcan Foundry in Lancashire in 1913. These elegant Edwardian beauties were the last examples of this rare wheel arrangement left on earth, and their subsequent breaking-up has left a missing link in the preservation of the principal phases of steam locomotive evolution.

The classic Uruguayan Mogul. This locomotive was the first example of the 28-strong N class Edwardian Moguls built by Beyer Peacock between 1906 and 1910. In common with their Paraguayan counterparts, these all-purpose engines have performed superbly for over three-quarters of a century and were one of the types that brought the steam age to a close in Paraguay during the early 1990s.

Above: The Surabaya steam tram was one of Java's most extraordinary railways. By the mid-1970s the tram ran from Wonokromo-Kota to the colourful market at Benteng, frequently halting while impromptu market stalls were removed from the track, its shrill, piercing whistle vainly endeavouring to inject a sense of urgency into the proceedings. Built by Beyer Peacock in Manchester in 1900, B1221 stands amid the market at Benteng. Opposite: A Beyer Peacock works picture of an 0-4-0 tram engine built for Java's Samarang–Joana Tramway in 1882. The motion was covered by 'skirts' for obvious safety reasons.

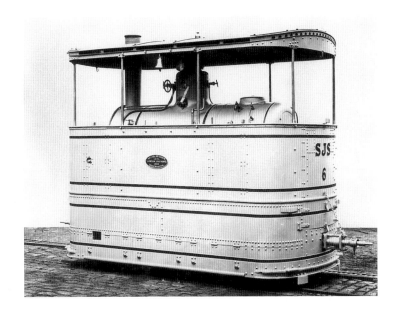

THE tram engine was one of the most fascinating variations ever developed from the conventional steam locomotive. From the 1880s they proliferated in two distinct types of use: the urban tramway that would occupy part of the road to serve central and suburban areas of towns and cities; and the roadside tramway which threaded its way into the countryside, sometimes as part of a major or national railway system.

Tram engines were produced by European builders both for home and export. The British builder Beyer Peacock of Gorton in Manchester was a prolific manufacturer, building over 200 examples between 1881 and 1910. Although most of these had vertical boilers and geared drive, the 97 they exported to Java had locomotive-type boilers.

As part of the Dutch East Indies until 1949, Java had many roadside tramways, a practice derived from Holland. The most fascinating of the many Javan systems was the one from Karangpilang to Benteng, which began in the countryside and ran though the teeming suburbs of Surabaya to the docks that connect with the ferry to Madura Island. It eventually closed because of one too many mishaps with the teeming road traffic. The unthinking switch to road transportation, partly as a result of Western influence, has brought Java's rich tradition of rural country railways to an end.

In Britain, much-loved systems like the Welsh narrow gauge Glyn Valley Tramway and the standard gauge Wisbech & Upwell in Cambridgeshire are but a distant memory. The last tram engines to soldier on were some of the former Great Eastern Railway's 0-6-0 trams, which survived on the East Anglian dock lines at Great Yarmouth, Lowestoft and Ipswich until 1955.

SUNSETS AND RAILWAY PHOTOGRAPHY

One of the handsome Moguls built by Borsig of Berlin in 1911 for the former Baghdad Railway wanders on to the pier at Hisaronu on Turkey's Black Sea coast.

RAILWAY photography has a long and celebrated history, spanning almost one and a half centuries. Although the majority of the millions of images taken have been the work of amateurs, many celebrated names have emerged and their collections survive as valuable social documents. Until the 1960s, the great majority of photographs were in black and white, so limiting the expression that could be given. This is especially sad when one considers the vibrant and imaginative colour schemes applied to trains around the world, epitomized by Carlisle in pre-grouping Britain where trains of seven companies ran into the Citadel station, each in a vivid, contrasting colour scheme, accentuated by the highly varied styles of the locomotives themselves.

When the livery of train are skilfully combined with the colour of its environment – as was beautifully done in the paintings of C. Hamilton Ellis – railway photography can become an art form. The correlation of a sunset and steam train renders this relationship in its most simplistic terms, although paradoxically the silhouette of a train 'blacks out' any colour, as revealed in the accompanying pictures. So simple is the combination of train and sunset that it has become over popularized and bowdlerized, a quick fix atmospheric picture. However, sensitively done, it offers limitless expression.

In its more serious manifestation, the sunset can add an allegorical element of impending demise, symbolizing decline or final hours. My picture, The Last Sunset, depicting a Nasmyth Wilson 2-8-0 in the scrapyards of Jamalpur works in northern India, is thematic, as is a study I made of one of the last survivors of the once 6,500-strong German Kriegsloks ambling through the Slovenian countryside against a blood-red flare of the dying sun – testimony to the last of a great breed.

A sunrise scene in the locomotive depot yard at Burdwan on the eastern region of Indian Railways. The engines are, left to right: XC class No. 22213 (Vulcan Foundry, 1929); XC class Pacific No. 22211 (Vulcan Foundry, 1929) and WG class Mikado No. 8177 (Canadian Locomotive Works, 1959).

A sunset scene of great impact photographed in a painterly way with harmonious forms and superb atmospheric contrasts. The train is a 'mixed' – a combination of freight and passenger vehicles. These were a common feature of many secondary lines around the world and usually ran infrequently, making them more of a challenge for the photographer.

The open firebox doors giving a dramatic glow to the cab indicate that the fireman is at work on a London & North Western Railway Claughton as it heads the Irish mail towards London. Twenty of these lovely engines were later rebuilt with large boilers, so creating the ultimate in LNWR express passenger types.

The depiction of trains in colour has been almost entirely the preserve of the photographer until relatively recent times. And over the most vibrant years of the Industrial Revolution surprisingly few painters took up overtly railway subjects. Relatively few artists concentrated on the industrial scene, and in Britain, despite the Victorian devotion to technology and the benefits it bestowed, it was seldom celebrated on canvas. F.G. Stephens, writing in the pre-Raphaelite journal *Art and Poetry* in May 1850, appealed for technological motifs, with little response, and certainly not from the pre-Raphaelites themselves.

The advent of colour photography and the availability of increasingly excellent cameras and film, combined with rising disposable income and more leisure time, have drastically changed the way we depict the world around us, although the most pictorial industrial subjects had passed into history by this time.

In recent years the dearth of colour pictures relating to historic railways has been partially made good by the photography of preserved railways. These depict trains and railway environments restored to the splendour of a century ago, whilst the dwindling steam age across the world has now been well recorded in colour, as revealed in the wide variety of pictures in this book.

THE MAJESTIC CREATIONS OF KARL GÖLSDORF
Austria's engineer extraordinaire

THE legendary Karl Gölsdorf, Chief Mechanical Engineer of the Austrian State Railway from 1891 until 1916, was a giant among locomotive engineers; he has been credited with some 60 different designs of locomotive for every conceivable purpose, ranging from two-cylinder compound 0-6-0s to four-cylinder compound 2-12-0s.

There is a majestic beauty about Gölsdorf locomotives which has never been bettered, and his family of designs is one of the most distinctive in the history of railways. Many of his creations were built in huge numbers, originally as compounds, but following the advent of superheating these were converted to simples. Many Gölsdorf engines had twin domes with a connecting pipe in order to give maximum steam space.

Gölsdorf engines were used by almost every railway in the Austro-Hungarian Empire. They also ran in other European countries such as Poland, Russia, Turkey and Sweden, and many thousands were built during the first quarter of the twentieth century. In later years many were built by the emergent countries following the break-up of the Austro-Hungarian Empire.

As C. Hamilton Ellis wrote, 'to British eyes Gölsdorf locomotives looked at first grotesque, but when one became used to them they were imposing indeed.' Not everyone would concur with that accommodating view, but in common with many locomotives created by the more innovative engineers, these Austrian machines were highly original.

Above: A Yugoslav State Railway (JZ) Class 153 2-6-0 tank, designed by Gölsdorf for the Austrian State Railway, surviving in industrial service in Slovenia in 1972.
Opposite: A Yugoslav State Railway (JZ) 28 class 0-10-0 at work between Jesenice and Nova Gorica. These magnificent engines were originally the Austrian State Railway's 80 class and when built were two-cylinder compounds.

Right: One of Goldsdorf's 2-8-2 rack and adhesion tanks as running in Romania after the splitting up of the Austro-Hungarian Empire.

Below: Rotting away amid the locomotive graveyards at Salonika lies this handsome giant, a 2-10-0 from Skoda, built to the design of the old Austrian Südbahn 580 class, classified La by the Greek State Railway.

Gölsdorf classics amid the locomotive graveyard at the old station in Salonika in northern Greece. In the foreground a 2-10-0 from Skoda built to the design of the old Austrian Südbahn 580 class is seen against a bevy of 0-10-0s descended from Gölsdorf's two-cylinder compound Class 180 of 1900. These Greek engines are part of a batch of 50 ordered from StEG in Vienna during the mid-1920s and classified Kb by the Greek State Railways.

RUSSIA'S GLORIOUS DAYS OF STEAM

RUSSIA is one of the world's greatest railway nations, but it is largely undocumented as publications within the former Soviet Union were tightly controlled and foreigners were not given access to railway installations. Even photography from station platforms was not tolerated.

Recent political changes in Russia have led to better access and understanding of its fascinating railway network, and it is now known that several thousand steam locomotives remain, albeit principally in strategic reserves. Following the modernization programme, many steam locomotives were greased-up and mothballed.

Other countries have done this to a limited extent, notably neighbouring Finland, but nowhere has the practice been so extensive as Russia. These reserves also exist in the former Communist satellite countries.

Though vast, Russia, like China, has pursued a policy of locomotive standardization, and as Russia's railways have been unified since Tsarist times this has been easy to develop. The decisison to abandon steam was not taken until 1955 – the same year as in Britain. At that time

Above: Two Soviet P36 4-8-4s at Skovorodino on the trans-Siberian route in 1970. These engines made a fine sight at the head of important trains such as Moscow–Leningrad and Moscow–Minsk–Brest.
Right: The magnificence of the Russian Railways Class P36 4-8-4 is captured in this night scene taken in the Ukraine in 1994. Built at Kolomna, a total of 251 P36s were put into service between 1950 and 1956.

Opposite: A Soviet Class P36 4-8-4 heads east for the 70-hour run to Vladivostok. The train of the Soviet Union and latterly Russia that everyone knows is the Trans-Siberian express, on which man and machine work in the most adverse of conditions.

Above: A USSR class P36 4-8-4 pauses at Skovorodino with train No. 1, the westbound Khabarovsk–Moscow express in November 1970. This train covered a distance of some 6,000 miles (9,600km). At this time, many of the passenger trains on the trans-Siberian route were operated by relays of P36s, in what was the last big steam operation in the Soviet Union.

Russia was largely dependent on steam, with an estimated 36,000 engines active on the 5ft (1524mm) gauge. Most were built to several basic designs.

The first major standardization occurred with the O class 0-8-0s of which 9,500 were built between 1891 and 1923, but these were to be exceeded by the E class 0-10-0s, which, with variations, totalled some 13,000 locomotives to qualify as the most numerous steam design of all time. Other grand designs include the So class 2-10-0s, with an estimated 5,000 built between 1934 and 1954, and the post-war L class 2-10-0s, which totalled upwards of 5,000 examples. All of these are freight-hauling classes which constituted the great majority of locomotives, but the standard S class 2-6-2 passenger engines, which were derived from the Italian fast passenger 2-6-2s, reached a total of 3,750, by far the most numerous passenger class to run in Russia.

Virtually no steam survives in main line service, but many reserve engines are steamed once a year for tests. Examples of classes L, E and Su are still to be found, along with other types, although it would seem that the changing political climate has led to many reserve engines being scrapped, to raise desperately needed cash. This process will almost certainly continue and the future of these reserves is now in question.

SENTINELS *Economical, hardworking and flexible*

SENTINEL locomotives were a product of the Sentinel Waggon Works at Shrewsbury in Shropshire and were introduced in 1923. They were superheated and had vertical boilers and cylinders with chain drive and geared transmission. The 'superiority' of the Sentinel, which was used mainly for shunting, light passenger work and goods trains at modest speeds, lay mainly in the design of the boiler, the main advantage being that coal consumption was half that of conventional locomotives.

They were built in various gauges, ranging from 2ft 6in (762mm) to 5ft 6in (1676mm), and from 80hp for light industrial use to 200hp articulated types. Some of the earliest 80hp Sentinels were sent to India where they were used on the irrigation schemes that created such fecundity in the Punjab. Here they were put to work hauling up to 42 hopper wagons up gradients of 1 in 110, doing three times the work previously done by a petrol tractor and at one-third of the cost.

In England these machines were used widely on public works contracts where they were found capable of hauling 10 fully loaded wagons up a 1 in 16.5 gradient. In Kenya some 80hp Sentinels were fuelled with sisal poles and, in spite of the poor calorific value of such fuel, were able to pull a load of 30 tons up a 1 in 28 gradient.

In Egypt 100hp Sentinels were employed in working passenger trains on that country's 2ft 5½in (750mm) gauge Egyptian Delta Light Railways, where they could be seen hauling up to six carriages. As well as seeing service in Australia, New Zealand, France, Ceylon, Denmark, Sweden, South Africa, Iraq, Peru, Spain and Brazil, they were also used in Britain: the large 200hp machines were used by the London & North Eastern Railway for shunting. The company also had a fleet of Sentinel railcars, some of which were named.

Between 1923 and 1957, Sentinel manufactured over 850 locomotives. In 1957 Rolls Royce paid £1.5 million for the 16-acre site in Shrewsbury.

From the 1920s onwards, Sentinel of Shrewsbury built a family of locomotives with vertical boilers. These engines represented a kind of halfway stage between steam and diesel, having been designed to utilise the full power of the boiler at any speed.

A Sentinel in industrial use on the Oxford Ironstone system at Wroxton near Banbury. Although Sentinels claimed their engines effected huge savings in coal, oil and maintenance compared with conventional industrial locomotives, it is surprising that relatively so few of them were built.

THE WORLD'S MOST NUMEROUS LOCOMOTIVE

CHINA'S QJ 2-10-2s were introduced in 1957, having been derived from the Russian Railway's LV Class and built with Soviet technical aid. They have been produced by six different works in China, but since the mid-1960s production has been centred on Datong. Upwards of 5,000 QJs have been built for service throughout China. They are powerful locomotives with a tractive effort of 63,340lb (28,730kg). One engine can haul 3,000-tonne trains over level routes, but so severe are the gradients on many lines that double-headed QJs are common and triple-headers are not unknown.

It is interesting that China has resisted the temptation to build a larger locomotive, preferring to keep to a standard design, which has no defects, rather than risk the cost and complexities of diversification. One is reminded of Britain's Midland Railway which over many years produced an endless stream of standard inside-cylinder 0-6-0s, which were invariably double-headed on the heavier trains. Again, in common with the Midland Railway 0-6-0s, the QJs are frequently seen in passenger service.

There were, however, several serious attempts to improve the basic QJ design, and experiments were conducted both at Datong and in Harbin, but once it became obvious that dieselization and electrification were the way forward, work was abandoned.

The QJs are one of the very few designs in world history that were being withdrawn and built at the same time – a few of the early examples being condemned before building ceased at Datong.

After the last QJs had been built, China embarked on a modernization programme, and by the early 1990s QJ withdrawals became regular. China's aim to eliminate steam from the national railway network by 1999 may be over ambitious, but the writing is now clearly on the wall, although some provincial lines which operate QJs will continue into the new century, including the spectacular new route running between Tongliao to Jining Nan, which includes the most spectacular steam operation left on earth.

A winter study of QJs on shed in Shenyang during the winter of 1991-2. Though China's most ubiquitous steam type, many variations of trim and colour occur throughout their ranks.

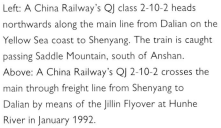

Left: A China Railway's QJ class 2-10-2 heads northwards along the main line from Dalian on the Yellow Sea coast to Shenyang. The train is caught passing Saddle Mountain, south of Anshan.
Above: A China Railway's QJ 2-10-2 crosses the main through freight line from Shenyang to Dalian by means of the Jillin Flyover at Hunhe River in January 1992.

THE TRUSTY BRITISH DRUDGE *Inside-cylinder 0-6-0s*

On 29 December 1976, when this picture was taken, former Indian Railways' SGC class 0-6-0 No. 34225 was the works' pilot at Jamalpur. Here the engine is caught taking a breather, having just hauled a mighty XE class Mikado into the scrap yard.

THE inside-cylinder 0-6-0 was one of the definitive forms of British locomotive. It was ideally suited to the concept of relatively light, frequent trains operating over well-maintained tracks. Though oriented towards being a freight hauler, it was often a mixed-traffic engine, especially on secondary routes.

The type first appeared on the Leicester & Swannington Railway during the 1830s and remained in production for almost a century, the last examples being Oliver Bulleid's war-time Q1 Austerities for the Southern Railway, which were built in 1942.

Virtually all of Britain's innumerable railway companies had inside-cylinder 0-6-0s, all of them delightfully and subtlety different. None the less one or two proven standard types could have done the work of all of them equally well.

The 0-6-0 formed the first major standardization programme in locomotive history with Ramsbottom's London & North Western Railway DXs, an incredible total of 943 engines being built over the years 1858 to 1872. His successor, Francis Webb, followed the 0-6-0 tradition keenly with his 17 inch goods and later mixed-traffic 'Cauliflowers'. Some of Webb's inside-cylinder 0-6-0s were even known to handle Anglo-Scottish expresses in their early years on the section between Crewe and Carlisle.

The Midland Railway was another devotee of 0-6-0s, to the extent that if one of them was not powerful enough, two were readily provided. They reigned supreme throughout Kirtley's and Johnson's tenures as chief mechanical engineers. Indeed Johnson's 4Fs of 1911 continued to be built after the grouping by the LMS until as late as 1940. It may be said that, like the sorcerer's apprentice who could not stop making broom sticks, Derby works could not stop building inside-cylinder 0-6-0s.

Above: The LMS 4Fs were the last in a long and noble line of inside-cylinder 0-6-0s, which began with the Midland Railway in the middle of the nineteenth century. The 4Fs were introduced by the Midland Railway in 1911 and building continued after the grouping under the LMS until 1940, by which time 772 were in service.

Left: The former Great Central Railway J11 Pom-Pom inside-cylinder 0-6-0s were powerful and free-steaming. They were introduced by J.G. Robinson in 1901 and one is seen here at Nottingham Victoria station in BR days. Note the remarkable similarity between this engine and the Indian SGC on the opposite page.

WORKHORSE OF THE LOGGING RAILWAYS *Shays*

THESE remarkable locomotives were the brainchild of Ephraim Shay, a backwoods logging engineer. In common with the Garratt, the Shay became associated with one particular locomotive builder, in this case Lima of Ohio, which took out a patent on the design. The Shay was particularly an engine of the America Pacific Northwest, being designed to work over logging railways where tracks are lightly or tentatively built, steeply graded, tightly curved, badly maintained and often embedded in a muddy quagmire.

Under such conditions, running speed becomes subordinate to good articulation and an efficient transmission of power. To achieve this, Shays are flexibly mounted on four-wheel bogies, known as trucks. The cylinders, usually two or three in number, are set alongside each other in a vertical position ahead of the cab on the engine's right-hand side. These cylinders drive a horizontal crankshaft running the entire length of the engine, the drive being applied by pinions slotted into bevelled gears on the truck wheels. The single crankshaft is made flexible by incorporating universal joints placed at intervals throughout its length. The gearing ratio applied to the small wheels gives an even turning movement and prevents slipping.

Almost 3,000 Shays were built, principally by Lima, many being exported to various parts of the world where they worked over a variety of gauges. The last examples left in commercial service were in the Philippines, where survivors lingered until the early 1990s.

Above: Lima of Ohio took out a patent on the Shay and this works' picture of a three-cylinder, three truck example reveals the cylinders, the horizontal crankshaft and its bevelled gear connection with the wheels on the trucks. The cylinders and drive were traditionally set on the engine's right-hand side and boiler was displaced to compensate.
Right: A number of Shays are still active on preserved railroads, including 1916 Lima-built 3-truck Shay No. 14, formerly West Side Lumber Co., seen here in October 1993 passing under the famed 96ft-high Devil's Gate viadiuct on the Georgetown Loop in the Rocky Mountains to the west of Denver.

Shays with their geared drive were developed for lightly laid, undulating logging lines. They could work in conditions which no conventional engine would tolerate.

Twin Seams Mining Company's Shay No. 5 was caught hard at work at Kellerman, Alabama, in September 1962. The crankshaft linked by universal joints can be clearly seen.

LOCOMOTIVE REPAIR AND RESTORATION

An Edwardian view of England's North Eastern Railway works at Darlington, which was the principal location for building and overhauling the company's locomotives. An 0-4-4 light passenger tank engine is seen on the overhead crane along with one of the company's ubiquitous inside-cylinder 0-6-0s.

ONE of the many inherent problems with the steam locomotive was its low availability compared with more modern forms of motive power. This manifested itself in various ways: lighting-up, steam raising, routine coaling and watering, turning and fire-raking were time-consuming daily chores, while boiler washing, though not a daily activity, significantly reduced an engine's availability for traffic.

Although much routine maintenance was carried out at the engine's home running shed, heavy overhauls required locomotives going away to workshops every 150,000 miles (240,000km) or so. They would be away for anything up to six weeks, having been stripped down to their bare frames in the case of the heaviest overhauls as boilers, fireboxes, cylinders, wheels and running gear were restored following thousands of miles of heavy stresses and wear imposed by working heavy loads.

In Britain these works were located in the traditional railway towns like Derby, Crewe, Doncaster and Swindon, and engines were invariably built and overhauled in the same complex. Around the world this was not usually the case, and in developing areas such as Africa and Latin America, locomotive works often appeared far away from developing areas. In the case of Location Works in Ghana, for example, they appeared like a segment of industrial Lancashire grafted on to African jungle. In China, Russia and the US, locomotive building was invariably separate from the rank-and-file process of routine shopping.

A China Railway Pacific undergoes periodic overhaul at Changchun locomotive works in northern China as an ex-works QJ 2-10-2 acts as yard pilot in the background. Changchun's locomotive works employs 5,000 people and undertakes 300 major steam locomotive overhauls each year.

THE GHOST THAT REFUSED TO DIE *Mallet No.7*

Top: An American 0-6-6-0 four-cylinder compound Mallet alongside one of the last vertical-cylinder Shays at the Maaslud Exchange sidings at the Insular Lumber Logging Co., Fabrica, on the Philippine island of Negros. Above: Dawn over the Insular Lumber Company's sawmill reveals the contours of a Lima two-truck Shay raising steam for a day's work.

THE Insular Lumber Company's logging railway, based on Fabrica on the island of Negros in the Philippines, was home to the world's most incredible steam survivor. Built by Baldwin in 1925, the company's 0-6-6-0 four-cylinder compound Mallet No. 7 had a chequered life and was widely regarded as a possessed engine; apart from the almost daily breakdowns and derailments, innumerable people were killed by the engine and it was involved in two serious accidents.

One night, after heavy rains, thousands of tons of earth and rock gave way, throwing No. 7 into the river-bed far below. Such was the Mallet's value to the company that the locomotive was dismantled where it lay and the pieces hauled back up to track level. In another disaster, the rear four log cars in a train it was hauling broke away. Discovering the mishap, the driver came to a stop on a high American-style trestle bridge. The ever-accelerating breakaway log cars caught up, smashing the train into the ravine below and killing 50 people who were illicitly riding the logs.

Seeing No. 7 at night was an unforgettable experience. With wood sparks curling off her smoke stack and leaking steam from all cylinders, the enormous mahogany-burning Mallet trundled at an average 10 mph (16km/h), her silhouette constantly changing in the ghostly patterns created by the fire and swirling steam. The grotesque noises from the four leaking cylinders and the hollow rasps of her uneven exhaust seemed appropriate for her reputation. There were few places in the world where one could see an 0-6-6-0 compound Mallet alongside one of the last vertical-boilered Shays.

No. 7 was kept going by parts ingeniously manufactured in the company's workshop. Philippine sugar mills were accustomed to a make-do-and-mend approach to repairs. But over the years, as the boiler grew progressively weaker, the steam pressure was dropped until the engine could haul only a fraction of the tonnage it could manage in its prime. No. 7 now lies abandoned in the encroaching jungle, alongside one of the system's Lima-built Shays.

Seven years after the picture on the opposite page was taken, a further expedition to Negros revealed No. 7 abandoned and weed-strewn. The Insular Lumber system had closed and the engine, along with Shay No. 12, was dumped close to the Sagay sugar central complex at Bato. The picture was taken on 17 December 1981.

THE FABULOUS GARRATTS *Evolutionary offshoots*

THE Garratt is perhaps the most important evolutionary offshoot of main line steam locomotive development. Herbert William Garratt, an English engineer, took out a patent on the principle in 1907, and shortly afterwards Beyer Peacock of Manchester took up his idea. Unfortunately, Garratt died in 1913, at the age of 49, and although he lived long enough to see the first fruits of his idea exported from England, he was never to know the great contribution he had made to steam locomotive development.

The Garratt was conceived at exactly the right time. As railways developed, the problem arose of how to operate increasingly heavy trains over the steeply graded, curved and lightly laid routes, which, out of economic necessity, had to be laid when countries were first opened up. The Garratt perfectly addressed this problem by using two sets of wheels and motion, which were articulated. The boiler and firebox could therefore be built to whatever size was necessary because they are free of wheels and axles. Conversely, as the wheels are free of the boiler, they too could be made to whatever diameter was considered best. One water tank was mounted ahead of the boiler, with a combined fuel and water unit to the rear. Cylinders are placed at the far ends of these units, both of which are articulated from the boiler. This provides the maximum adhesion, but spreads the weight over a long area.

Lack of restriction in firebox design meant that it could also be built deeply for maximum combustion. This is a great advantage when consuming the poor quality coal, while the fat, and characteristically, short boiler facilitates rapid steaming since the short tube lengths provide efficient heat transference. The slogging pugnacity with which Garratts undergo their duties is a tribute to these aspects of the design, creating a locomotive capable of moving heavy loads over difficult lines.

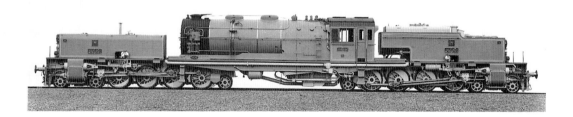

Top: An Iranian State Railway 4-8-2+2-8-4 Garratt. Four of these giants were delivered from Beyer Peacock in 1936 for working the northern section of the main line which crosses the Elburz mountains with grades of 1 in 36.
Above: One of the magnificent 4-8-2+2-8-4 Garratts supplied after World War II by Beyer Peacock to the FCAB Antofagasta (Bolivia) and Chile Railway, which reached the highest altitude of any railway in the world – 15,814ft.
Right: A pair of Zimbabwe Railways Class 14A 2-6-2+2-6-2 Garratts storm Mulungwane Bank on the Bulawayo–West Nicholson line in 1992. Eighteen of these locomotives were built by Beyer Peacock of Manchester in 1953–4.

THE FABULOUS GARRATTS

Upwards of 2,000 Garratts have been built for a multiplicity of purposes, over a wide range of gauges. Helped by British colonial markets, Garratts spread to many parts of the world – the Indian subcontinent, Australia, New Zealand and Latin America – where they were well suited to rugged terrain and difficult operating conditions. But it was Africa that they truly colonized, much as their articulated relations, the Mallets, had colonized America.

The largest Garratt ever built went to Russia – a solitary engine with a 20-ton axle loading, designed to haul 2,500 tons. Equally impressive were the East African metre gauge Class 59 4-8-2+2-8-4s, weighing 252 tons in full working order. These magnificent beasts worked the 332-mile (531km) drag between Mombassa on the Indian Ocean and the Kenyan capital of Nairobi. East African Railways proposed an even larger Garratt, at 372 tons, with a 27-ton axle load. This giant 4-8-4+4-8-4 would have been breathtaking to see in operation, but traffic levels proved less buoyant than expected and the Class 59s so efficient that the proposed Class 61 was never required.

Several classes of Garratts can still be found in industrial use in South Africa and on neighbouring Zimbabwe's main line, although here they are now relegated to shunting and tripping duties.

Above: One of the most dramatic British locomotive designs was the 2-6-0+0-6-2 Garratt, 33 of which were built by Beyer Peacock for the London Midland & Scottish Railway between 1927 and 1930. Apart from the single London & North Eastern Garratt, they were the only main line Garratts to run in Britain. Breaking up of the class began in 1955, and by 1958 they had all gone.

Left: The versatility of the Garratt and its application to a wide variety of gauges is evident in this scene in Beyer Peacock's works at Gorton, Manchester. Gauges of Garratts around the world have ranged from 2ft (610mm) on the Tasmanian Government Railways to 5ft 6in (1676mm) on both India's Bengal Nagpur Railway and Spanish National Railways.

Below: The nameplate from one of East African Railway's 59 class 4-8-2+2-8-4 Garratts. Thirty-four of these 250-ton giants plied the Mombasa to Nairobi line, which includes 1 in 60 grades and climbs the equivalent of a mile in altitude between the coast and Nairobi. *Mount Kilimanjaro*, numbered 5928, was built by Beyer Peacock of Manchester in 1955.

SHUNTING LOCOMOTIVE TYPES

Sudan Railway's locomotive works at Atbara had this splendid Hunslet 0-6-0 tank as works' pilot. It was built in 1951 and was caught here against one of the ranging sunsets of the Nile on 30 December 1982.

THE most common shunting type – or switcher, as they were known in the US – was the 0-6-0 tank which offered the necessary power and adhesion for most applications. Tank engines were equally mobile for moving backwards and forwards with the weight of their fuel bearing directly on to the driving wheels, helping to provide the necessary adhesion for moving long rakes of wagons. Tender engines were cumbersome and offered no advantage: only limited amounts of coal were needed for yard work, and water could easily be taken between bouts of shunting.

For light work in smaller yards, which often had tight curves and restricted spaces, the 0-4-0 tank was the preferred type, whilst for heavier applications the 0-8-0 was adopted. In the US, the 0-6-0 and 0-8-0 switcher appeared in tender form more frequently than elsewhere, often with tenders which were designed in a wedge-shape for clear vision when running backwards.

Many famous shunting types have evolved. One of the first was Ramsbottom's 0-6-0 Special Tanks, which were introduced on Britain's London & North Western Railway in the 1860s. In Germany, the Prussian State Railways had their T3 0-6-0 well tank, of which upwards of 1,500 were built, along with the larger T13 0-8-0T which numbered some 700 examples.

Shunting was often carried out – especially during the twentieth century – by downgraded main liners. This was particularly true in Britain where generations of inside-cylinder 0-6-0s, whose life in main line service had come to an end, were given a new lease of life shunting. The same was true in North America, where downgraded main liners of medium power and small wheels became switchers. Almost anything could be pressed into yard

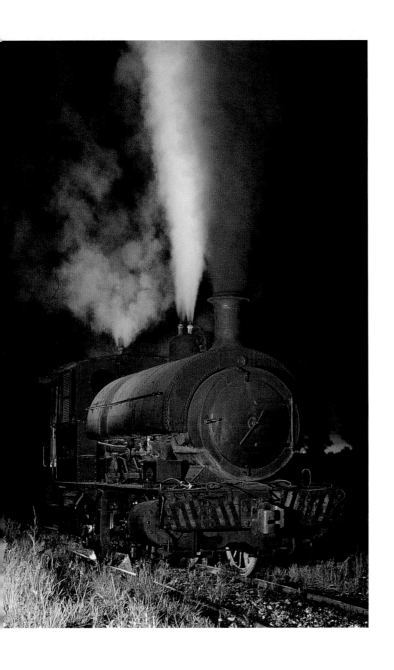

Above left: This delightful Sharp Stewart 0-4-0 saddle tank of 1903 was one of a varied roster at the Cosim steelworks at Mogi das Cruzes near São Paulo. Above right: Another veteran on the Cosim steelworks roster was this magnificent Baldwin 0-6-2 saddle tank, built in November 1896 to the 5ft 6in (1676mm) gauge for Brazil's Paulista Railway. She was pensioned off into industrial service in 1944. This American switcher makes a fine contrast with the British Sharp Stewart 'Scottish' Pug alongside.

SHUNTING LOCOMOTIVE TYPES

Above: At one time, the pannier tank could be seen almost anywhere on the Great Western (latterly the Western Region of BR). Equally at home on short passenger trains or goods workings, they lasted almost until the end of steam.
A pannier simmers in a yard taking a breather between duties.
Below: Reading A-5A 0-4-0 No. 1168, built in 1907, shunts at Atlantic City, New Jersey, on 12 October 1935.

A China Railway's industrial SY Mikado works amid temperatures of −25°C at the Zalainoer open-cast colliery system at Manzhouli alongside the Russian border in north-eastern China.

service; one of the most remarkable examples was the last ten examples of India's 5ft 6in (1676mm) gauge express passenger XC class Pacifics, which ended their days allocated to Burdwan in Bengal for heavy shunting work.

The encroachment of main line engines into shunting service throughout much of the twentieth century tended to limit the evolution of the shunting engine proper. Another contributory factor occurred during the 1930s, when diesels began to make their presence felt. They provided many obvious advantages over steam such as easy manoeuvrability, an excellent torque for moving heavy loads, the ability to perform long periods of uninterrupted service without returning to depots for maintenance, and the ability to shut down during periods of idleness and quickly start up again when needed.

THE 2-10-0, or Decapod, first appeared on America's railroads during the 1890s. It was not widely used, the direct gravitation to Santa Fe 2-10-2s being preferred, and less than 700 Decapods were built for America's railroads. Russia, which generally followed the US in locomotive practice, was a far larger user of 2-10-0s, which first appeared there in 1915. Many thousands were put into service, embracing sevceral different classes, including some of the German Kriegsloks, which were converted to Russia's 5ft (1524mm) gauge.

By World War I, Decapods were widespread in Europe, especially on the Prussian State Railways and the Austrian State Railways. Germany was by far the largest user of 2-10-0s, with its Class 44 three-cylinder examples, its Class 50 two-cylinder machines and the Kriegslok, which was a wartime version of the Class50. These three classes alone added up to over 12,000 locomotives

Very few 2-10-0s ever worked in Africa, Latin America or on the Indian subcontinent. This was because the type's tight rigidity was unsuitable for the rough and tumble encountered in these areas of the world. Even China saw few examples, the railway engineers there preferring the Mikado or Santa Fe.

Britain had to wait until World War II for its first 2-10-0s, which were in the form of Robin Riddle's War Department engines of 1943. The 2-10-0 truly came of age in Britain with the superb 9Fs, one of British Railways' twelve standard designs conceived after nationalization. The 9Fs totalled 251 engines and they consummated the 2-10-0 as a brilliant all-rounder, proving ideal for heavy mineral hauling, fast freight operation and even express work, on which they achieved speeds of 90mph (144km/h). British Railways' last steam locomotive, built in 1960, was to the 9F design and appropriately named *Evening Star*.

Opposite: Strasburg Railroad 2-10-0 No. 90 at Paradise, Pennsylvania on 9 February 1982. This was the last regular service Decapod in North America, and until the early 1960s worked on the Great Western Railroad in Colorado. Above: A Pennsylvania Railroad I-1sa 2-10-0 No. 4595 on Horseshoe Curve, Pennsylvania in the late 1930s. These were amongst the last Pennsylvania steam locomotives to survive, and some remained active until 1957, working 100-car coal drags with four engines per train.

Left: The German Kriegslokomotiv worked in many European countries, either through direct military action by Germany or in subsequent reparation packages. The Turkish State Railways had a batch of around 50, one of which is seen here in beautifully trimmed form, complete with Star and Crescent, at Afyon on 16 August 1976.

Below: A Pennsylvania Railroad I-1sa 2-10-0 No. 4595 on Horseshoe Curve, Pennsylvania in 1938. Introduced in 1916, 598 of these engines were built, principally by Baldwin, but some at the Pennsylvania's works in Altoona.

A brace of the Turkish State Railway's magnificent Skyliner 2-10-0s Nos 536374 and 56318, both built by the Vulcan Ironworks, Pennsylvania in 1947, at Lalabel on 6 November 1972.

Above: Some of the nameplates from condemned locomotives in the stores at Location Works following the abandonment of steam traction during the early 1980s. Tribes, slaving forts and British governors were all commemorated.
Below: Vulcan Foundry 4-8-2 No. 266 *Techiman* complete with Giesl chimney alongside the wood yard at the motive power depot in Accra.

VAST tracts of fever-laden jungles had to be penetrated by British engineers to build the Gold Coast's first railway through 150 miles (240km) of jungle and rain-forest, interspersed with mosquito-ridden pools and swamps. Malaria was rife. But if the reserves of gold in the interior were to be exploited, the railway had to be built.

The Gold Coast railways were a great source of pride: the railway developed the Gold Coast's vast potential for cocoa to found the Cadbury empire, whilst manganese from Nsuta, bauxite from Awaso and timber from Kumasi all flowed to the coast for export.

Passenger travel was luxurious. Within two decades of the dark country being opened up by railways, trains with restaurant and sleeping facilities were in service, and travellers could assuage their thirst with a bottle of Bass for 6d or whisky and soda for 9d.

The railway works at Location were like a piece of industrial Lancashire grafted on to primeval forests.

A pair of Vulcan Foundry 4-8-2s at rest beneath the coaling stage at the motive power depot in Accra. 1954 was the last full year of steam operation in the Gold Coast, with 141 locomotives on the country's active roster, 62 of which were 4-8-2s. The example here is fitted with a Giesl chimney, a latter-day improvement to steam locomotives.

Everywhere one looked were artefacts from Britain's days as the workshop of the world: machine tools from Somerskills of Sowerby Bridge and Smiths of Glasgow, anvils from Brooks of Lye and clocks from Gents of Leicester to name but a few. Inevitably magnificent British locomotives accompanied the tools to maintain them: 4-8-2s from the Vulcan Foundry in Lancashire, 4-6-0s from Robert Stephenson's works in Darlington, Pacifics from Beyer Peacock in Manchester and some heavy duty 0-8-0 tanks from Hunslet of Leeds.

Another wonderful British tradition was the naming of locomotives which commemorated tribes, British governors and the infamous forts from which slaves were conveyed to the United States.

In the years following independence, Ghana Railways fell into decline and almost shut down. A rescue plan was embarked upon in the mid-1980s, but this found no place for steam, despite the fact that the complexities of diesel-electrics were far from ideal for Ghanaian conditions and steam could, and should, have been retained. It is doubly sad that the Ghanaians did not embark on any preservation of their railway heritage.

Opposite: The steam locomotive shed at Kumasi following
closure with Vulcan Foundry 4-8-2 No. 277 *Dagomba*, which was
the last steam locomotive delivered to the Ghana Railways.
Below: The frame and wheels of Vulcan Foundry Class 130 4-8-2
E.M. Bland in the overgrown shed yard at Kumasi. The engine's
boiler has been removed and sold out of railway service to provide
steam at a local saw mill.

THE Prairie 2-6-2 was a logical extension of the Mogul, the additional axle allowing a bigger boiler and deeper firebox. The type, which came into production in the United States in the 1900s, appeared most commonly as a general mixed-traffic engine, but it also occurred with wheel diameters as great as 6 ft 8 inches (203cm) for fast passenger work.

The Prairie assumed huge importance in Russia, where it was introduced in 1911. Typically American in concept, their S/Su classes were built over a 40-year period and eventually totalled 3,750 examples, becoming the country's principal passenger locomotive. The Prairie was also eagerly adopted by Italian Railways in the form of the high-stepping four-cylinder Class 685s of 1912: these eventually totalled some 390 examples.

Curiously, there were vast areas of the world in which the Prairie was either non-existent or rarely appeared, such as Africa, Latin America and the Indian subcontinent.

One of the greatest Prairies was Gresley's three-cylinder V2 class, which was introduced on the London & North Eastern Railway in 1936. These engines proved superb both for mixed-traffic and express passenger work and eventually totalled 184 examples. Known as 'the engines that won the war', on account of their prodigious feats in hauling passenger trains of up to 25 coaches, they were also extremely fast.

Most British Praires, however, were used for suburban and branch line trains, which called for good acceleration from the frequent stops as well as the ability to pull anything up to nine or ten packed commuter carriages.

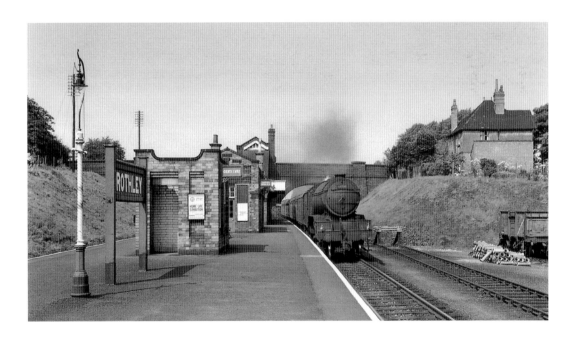

Left: The former Soviet Railways utilised the 2-6-2 type for most passenger trains during the steam era. Here, Su class No 251.86 is seen near Novograd in February 1995.

Above: A Gresley three-cylinder V2 2-6-2 storms southward through Rothley on the Great Central main line. This railway, opened in 1899, was intended to be part of a continental loading-gauge through route between the industrial cities of northern England and those of Europe via a Channel tunnel upon which work had commenced.

RIVALRY ACROSS THE BORDER

BRITAIN'S main lines are both numerous and varied in character; each has its geographical distinctiveness and famous topographical views. These, combined with the architecture of the pre-grouping companies, renders each route an experience to be savoured. Most of the shorter main lines were originally operated by one company, but in the case of the three Anglo-Scottish ones, various companies were involved, each with their richly varied locomotive traditions.

It was inevitable that rivalry would exist between the East and West Coast routes. This reached fever pitch during the railway races of 1895 when trains raced thought the night between London and Aberdeen. The converging point for the two routes was Kinnaber Junction, north of Montrose. North from here it was joint running over the Caledonian main line into Aberdeen. These incredible races have formed some of the greatest legends in railway history and resulted in a time of 8 hours and 32 minutes for the 540 miles (864km) from Euston to Aberdeen. This represents a continuous average of over 60 mph (96km/h) – little slower than present-day timing over a century later!

If the West Coast had presumed to have won the 1895

races, matters were redressed almost half a century later when Gresley's streamlined A4 *Mallard* achieved the world speed record for steam of 126 mph (201km/h) down Stoke Bank, whereas the best that Stanier's streamlined Pacific locomotive *Coronation* managed to achieve on the West Coast route was 114mph (182km/h).

In contrast, the Midland route was a much quieter and slower affair. It included the Settle to Carlisle section, one of Britain's most magnificent stretches of railway, which is now and will increasingly become, an international tourist attraction. It is incomprehensible that British Rail tried for years to close it.

Above: The up 'Thames-Clyde' express hauled by Royal Scot No. 46117 *Welsh Guardsman*. This painting, depicting a typical November afternoon, can be dated quite accurately, since the engine carries its new nationalized number, whereas its tender still shows its previous LMS ownership with the simplified sans serif letters used in the 1946 livery.
Left: The southbound 'Royal Scot' waits to leave Glasgow Central for London Euston behind Camden-allocated Pacific No. 46240 *City of Coventry*.

Gresley A4 class
Pacific No. 60011
Empire of India, an
Edinburgh
Haymarket engine,
arrives at the buffer
stops at King's
Cross with the non-
stop 'Elizabethan'
from Edinburgh.

EXPRESS TANKS AROUND THE WORLD

Coaling by mobile steam crane at Bandel shed on 12 December 1979. The engine is WT class 2-8-4 tank No. 14021, built at Chitteranjan locomotive works in Bengal in 1966.

VERY few of the world's racy-looking tanks were truly express engines. The type was not common and there were large parts of the world where such engines seldom or never appeared, such as Russia, China, America and Africa. One obvious disadvantage of tank engines for fast long-distance running was their lack of fuel capacity; there were also concerns that the surging of water in the side tanks at high speeds would cause instability.

Most express tanks occurred in Europe, and in Britain the London, Brighton & South Coast Railway began a tradition with their Class I3 4-4-2s of 1906, followed by 4-6-2 tanks in 1910 and in 1914 some magnificent Baltic 4-6-4s. These were followed in 1926 by the Southern Railway's 2-6-4 River tanks, but these were deemed unstable at speed.

The London & North Western also had some 4-4-2 tanks for suburban workings around London and Manchester and some 4-6-2 tanks built between 1910 and 1916 for longer distance work, 20 of them even having water scoops. In 1914, the Great Central introduced a class of 4-6-2s, which were sprightly in the best of Great Central traditions.

In Europe, Holland and Sweden had some fine examples, while the Austrian Südbahn Class 629s of 1917 were absolute masterpieces, providing the basis for the later Austrian State Railway 78 class 4-6-4s. The Prussian State Railways T18s, a tank version of the celebrated P8 4-6-0s, worked in a number of countries, including Poland and Turkey.

The last examples of this rare genera were built in India; the WM class 2-6-4s were built until 1954, but the very last examples were the fabulous WT 2-8-4Ts, 30 of which were built between 1959 and 1967, and examples of these racehorses are shown here.

Above: Tank locomotives are associated with mundane tasks, but the Baltic tanks of the LBSCR were given the job of hauling the prestigious all-Pullman 'Southern Belle'. Here No. 329 *Stephenson* drifts through the South Downs on its way to Brighton.

Below: The last express tank engine in service was WT class No 14011 (Chittaranjan works 1965). Allocated to Rajahmundry in Andhra Pradesh, it ended its days racing across the secondary lines around the Godavari Delta with lightly loaded trains.

Left: The overgrown yard at the once busy 5ft 6in (1676mm) gauge steam sheds inside the complex of Rohtas Industries. Just visible under the ever-encroaching vegetation are the system's two 0-6-0 tanks built by Jung of Jungenthal: in the foreground No. 12797 of 1957 and behind No. 11736 of 1953.

Above: Happier days at Rohtas Industries are revealed in this picture taken on 3 January 1977, showing the company's Kerr Stuart 0-4-0 saddle tank No. 4173 of 1921 alongside one of the beautiful Vulcan Foundry 0-6-4 suburban tanks, No. 3103 of 1915, which, along with a sister engine of 1908, was sold to Rohtas Industries in 1967.

DEHRI on Sone is a small town in Bihar located on the main line from Calcutta to New Delhi. It has become famous for the magnificent railway bridge over the River Sone, which was built by the British between 1856 and 1863 for the East Indian Railway. A truly inspired piece of civil engineering, the bridge is 4,726 feet (1440m) long and has 28 decks each spanning 157 feet (48m).

In more recent years the town has been celebrated as the base of Rohtas Industries, a huge industrial complex, which operated a 2ft 6in (762mm) system known as the Dehri Rohtas Light Railway. The company also had a 5ft 6in (1676mm) gauge system within the works complex for connection with Indian Railway's main line.

The Dehri Rohtas Light Railway was largely developed to carry limestone – cement being one of the company's products – and an amazing variety of locomotives was operated; virtually all were British and ranged from a Sentinel to various antiquated tank engines, none of which was more recent than the 1920s.

The 5ft 6in gauge roster was no less thrilling and included a pair of Edwardian-style 0-6-4 suburban tanks built in 1908 and 1915 for the East Indian Railways. Also present was a rare 0-4-0 saddle tank built by Kerr Stuart's California works at Stoke-on-Trent in 1921.

Maladministration closed the whole concern down; the railways were abandoned and the engines left to rot in the complex. The industry has been under legal review for many years, although hopes are still expressed that one day the system will return to life. In the meantime, the silent workshops and dust-laden offices with all furniture and equipment still in place provide an eerie accompaniment to the silent rusting locomotives.

FIREWORKS IN THE NIGHT SKY

Above: 'Bringing in the cane by Night'. This 1989 scene shows two bagasse-burning veterans at the Pesantren sugar mill in Java.
On the left is a four-cylinder compound 0-4-4-0 Mallet, built by Ducroo & Brauns in 1928, alongside No. 8 an 0-8-0 Klein Linder,
built by Orenstein & Koppel in 1922. The gauge at Pesantren is 700mm (2ft 3$^1/_2$in).
Opposite: A standard gauge Robert Stephenson & Hawthorn coal-fired 0-4-0 saddle tank brightens the night skies at Leicester
Power Station as it attempts to lift a rake of loaded wagons.

NIGHT-TIME heightens the steam locomotive's animated personality, and the sight of an open firebox door causing crimson reflections to dance in the smoke trail as flaming cinders shoot from the engine's chimney is a dramatic and beautiful manifestation of power. The phenomenon of fire-throwing applies to most steam locomotives when working hard; it was endemic on the London & North Western where relatively small engines were worked flat out with heavy trains, causing a constant shower of sparks.

The most spectacular fire-throwers are found in exotic areas of the world, where locomotive fuels are often light in nature. By far the most conducive is bagasse, the natural waste from sugar-cane processing. In a locomotive firebox, the straw-like substance explodes and large quantities are sucked off the fire bed and thrown out into the atmosphere, still burning.

The nutshell burners of Sumatra's palm oil plantations are also noted for their fiery effects. But most magnificent of all were the railways of the Paraguayan Chaco. These lines were built to carry quebracho logs for the production of tannin. Here, amid the deep blackness of the Chaco night, no trains needed a whistle as the engines throwing shrouds of crimson embers 30 yards into the air are visible from a distance of several miles; to see the ember-throwing veterans dragging their heavy trains to the factory, the track side shimmering in the vivid orange glow, constitutes steam railroading at its most magnificent. Here, in one of the remotest places on earth, the all-consuming magic of the steam train is personified.

Opposite: One of the amazingly decrepit Lima-built Shays, which lingered on the metals of the Insular Lumber Company on the Philippine Island of Negros. The engine undertakes its work-a-day chores around the coastal logging mill. Shrouds of teak sparks emanate from the chimney.

Above: This delightful American saddle tank was built by Baldwin in 1927. The engine was yard pilot at the railway works at Lavras in the state of Minas Gerais, Brazil. Known as the *Lavras Rose*, the engine is caught against a backdrop of banana groves.

Right: *Sally*, a 2ft (610mm) gauge Bagnall 0-4-0 saddle tank of 1930 takes a breather between duties on the Tipong Colliery network on the Indian coalfields of Upper Assam.

MOVING THE FREIGHT *Consolidations*

THE 2-8-0 was one of the principal forms of freight locomotive, and was found in most parts of the world. In some areas, like America and Russia, and to a lesser extent India, it flowered early to be replaced by more potent types; in other parts of the world, particularly Europe, 2-8-0s remained prevalent in a number of countries until the end of steam. This was especially true in Britain where many of the country's last steam locomotives were 2-8-0s built during the 1930s and 1940s.

Although the 2-8-0 did not appear on the world stage much before the start of the twentieth century, the type was used in North America as early as 1866, the first example in the United States being named *Consolidation*, by which tens of thousands of successors world-wide were to be generically known over the following hundred years.

By the turn of the century, the American 2-8-0 was in decline; it would have been replaced earlier had the general standard of track been capable of taking anything larger. However, 2-8-0s remained in many companies' rosters for secondary work over many more years.

The beginning of the twentieth century saw the 2-8-0 blossom in most areas of the world; it was built in huge numbers in Britain, starting in 1903 with Churchward's 28XXs for the Great Western. It formed part of the BESA standards for the Indian subcontinent of the same year, whilst France, Germany and the railways of the Austro-Hungarian Empire were 2-8-0 users.

Africa is the notable area of the world in which the 2-8-0 was all but absent. The light tracks, rough terrain and dubious fuels favoured such wheel arrangements as 4-8-0, 2-8-2 and 4-8-2, all of which had appeared on the continent's railways by the early years of the twentieth century.

This delightful Baldwin 2-8-0 was caught at work on the Pocogordo line of the Barcelos sugar mill in Campos State, Brazil. It was built by Baldwins in 1894, originally for main line use on Brazil's metre gauge network. Throughout Brazil, steam locomotives are referred to as 'Maria Fumacas'; translated this means 'Smoke Marys' – a name which seems to suit these American-styled engines to perfection.

A rake of mineral empties heads past Whissendine in the English Midlands, hauled by one of Stanier's celebrated ex-LMS 8F class 2-8-0s. Upwards of 800 of these locomotives were built during the 1930s and 1940s. Along with the WD 2-8-0s, which were a wartime version, they remained active until the end of steam in 1968.

DODO OF THE ATACAMA *The last Kitson Meyer*

Emitting a weird panting sound, the last surviving 0-6-0+0-6-0 Kitson Meyer clanks towards the camera near the Chilean port of Taltal with the golden hills of the Atacama Desert in silhouette from the setting sun. This solitary engine outlived the other nine examples of its type at Taltal, surviving until 1976, having been exported from Kitson of Leeds in 1907.

ONE of the world's most interesting steam survivors was the last Kitson Meyer articulated, which lingered at the port of Taltal on Chile's Pacific coast. The Kitson Meyers were a predecessor of the more successful Garratt and were used prolifically on the British-owned Gold and Nitrate railways of the Atacama Desert.

The Kitson Meyer is descended from the Meyer articulated, which was a large tank engine mounted on twin power bogies with the cylinders grouped at the inner ends of each bogie so that the steam feed pipe from the dome could be as short as possible. The Meyer possessed the disadvantage of having its firebox above the wheels, so restricting its depth, but it gained on the earlier Fairlie in having a normal position for the crew and better fuel-carrying capacity.

In the Kitson Meyer, which was developed by Kitsons of Leeds, the bogies were spread further apart and the firebox set between them, thereby avoiding the bad combination of ashes and the locomotive's motion. The cylinders were placed at the outer ends of each bogie so to allow space for a wide firebox.

In many cases, steam from the rear cylinders was exhausted from a separate chimney above the engine's bunker, which provided the amazing spectacle of dark smoke issuing from the leading chimney and shrouds of pure white steam from the rear one.

The Fairlies, Meyers, Kitson Meyers and Garratts all differed from the Mallet type, which was only a semi-articulated design with its rear set of wheels fixed as on a conventional locomotive.

The golden hills of the Atacama Desert provide a splendid foil as the last surviving Kitson Meyer steams into the port of Taltal on Chile's Pacific coast. The Kitson Meyer was superseded by the superior Garratt, and its construction was drastically curtailed. But for the advent of the Garratt, the Kitson Meyer would doubtless have become a prominent articulated type.

DISASTERS, WRECKS AND MISHAPS

The hole in the ground in Lindal. One of the world's most remarkable accidents occurred at Lindal on the Furness Railway at 08.15 on Thursday 22 September 1892, when underground colliery workings collapsed, creating a massive chasm on the railway down which fell Sharp Stewart six-coupled goods No. 115. At first the locomotive slid down a 30ft depression, but during the next few hours it fell further and further and was estimated to be about 200ft deep by 14.30. The engine was irretrievably buried for all time and it took a further six months completely to fill and consolidate the track-bed before trains could run again across Lindal sidings. From time to time thoughts have been expressed of retrieving so rare a prize.

WRECKS and mishaps are part of the railway's folklore. In the early days, one of the most common disasters was locomotive boilers exploding – often due to safety valves being tampered with by the engine crew in an effort to extract greater power. One particular incident occurred on 10 November 1840 when William Scaife and his fireman Joseph Rutherford were killed when the boiler of their locomotive, *Eclipse*, exploded at Bromsgrove station in Worcestershire. Both men were buried in the local churchyard, their graves being marked by headstones into which locomotives have been carved.

Wartime brings sabotage, one of the most telling examples being the wrecks lying in the Arabian desert thanks to the work of Lawrence of Arabia, described on pages 214–17.

Many locomotive wrecks lie under the sea, the engines having been on board ships that have sunk either by natural causes or by enemy action. An example of the latter is Truc Lagoon where at least one engine is clearly visible on the seabed. In Florida a locomotive disappeared off a branch line never to be seen again; after much searching, it was discovered that it had jumped the rails, plunged into a swamp and sunk without trace.

On 2 September 1892 in the Cumbrian village of Lindal, a brand new Furness Railway Sharp Stewart 0-6-0 slipped into a 30ft (9m) depression caused by mining subsidence. The driver, Thomas Postlethwaite, jumped clear from the engine, suffering only minor injuries. Over the next few hours the engine gradually sunk to some 200 feet (61m), before the hole caved in on top of it.

Right: Amid the tranquillity of Bromsgrove churchyard lies the graves of driver William Scaife and Fireman Rutherford of the Birmingham & Gloucester Railway, who were killed when the boiler of their locomotive exploded in Bromsgrove station on 10 November 1840. It is suspected that they had interfered with the engine's safety valve to build up greater steam pressure for the impending climb up the notorious 1 in 37 Lickey Bank.
Below: The wreck of *Khor Doniya*. Sudan Railway's North British-built Pacific No. 245 lies irretrievable at the foot of a large embankment, which gave way following heavy rains.

AMERICA'S UBIQUITOUS MOGULS

THE Mogul is one of the most celebrated and best-loved forms of locomotive. It lacked the cut and dash of the earlier 4-4-0 and later 4-6-0, but was excellent for mixed-traffic duties. It appeared in America as early as 1863 and found favour on the better engineered lines where its more limited flexibility did not present any difficulty.

Towards the end of the nineteenth century, as populations increased and industry grew, trains became heavier and the Mogul appeared for a while as a heavy freight hauler. In 1901, the Atchison Topeka & Sante Fe built some fascinating high-boilered examples with a wide firebox. By 1914 the power limit was approached with the Chicago & Western Indiana's examples producing a remarkable 36,000lb (16,329kg) of tractive effort.

Once the sheer weight of trains displaced it from main lines, the Mogul continued to be a favourite of many secondary and industrial lines. Large numbers of engines were downgraded into this kind of service, remaining evident virtually until the end of steam.

By its very nature the Mogul was a common export type and American Moguls have seen service in many parts of the world. Interestingly one was Britain, where in the 1900s, batches were supplied to several railways, at a time when UK builders had full order books.

Left: Mobile & Gulf Mogul No. 97 at Alabama in March 1966.
Opposite: This classic American Mogul was built by H.K. Porter of Pittsburg, Pennsylvania in 1919 and is seen here complete with yellow caboose at the Carlos Mañuel de Cepedes sugar mill in Camaguey Province on 20 April 1988. H.K. Porter was America's leading builder of industrial locomotives.

BY the early 1970s, steam had finished on the main lines of most Western countries and international attention was focused on what was left around the world. At that time the railways of eastern Europe were considered to be part of the strategic infrastructure of the Warsaw Pact and posed an often risky challenge for the railway photographer. With this in mind, several less sensitive countries came into the spotlight: India, Pakistan, South Africa and Turkey.

For Europeans, Turkey was the easiest to reach. It was cheap, relatively welcoming to visit and the rewards were abundant. In 1975 the country operated some 30 different classes, embracing a variety of exotic types from many builders, with a grand total of some 800 locomotives.

Turkey's historic allegiance with Germany was reflected in the railway and Prussian classic designs on its rosters such as the G8 0-8-0s, G8² 2-8-0s and G10 0-10-0s, along with the splendid suburban T18 4-6-4 tanks. Other German types included some extremely handsome 4-8-0s built by Henschel in the 1920s, augmented by a much more modern 2-10-2 of the early 1930s from Henschel, Krupp and Schwartzkopff.

Examples of all three leading designs of World War II were also on the active roster: Britain's Stanier 8F 2-8-0s; Germany's Kriegslokomotiv 2-10-0s; and Major Marsh's United States Army Transportation Corps S160 class 2-8-0s as well as some 'Middle East' Mikados.

French influence was in evidence with a batch of delightful 2-8-0s built by Humboldt of Paris in 1912. British influence, though limited, included some beautifully racy 2-8-2s built by Robert Stephenson's Newcastle works in 1929–32 for the Ottoman Railway. These engines were rare examples of exported British Mikados for passenger service.

A Bagnall 0-8-0 tank of 1937 waits for the ladles to fill with molten steel at Karabuk steelworks, Turkey. The Turkish hero Kemal Ataturk was instrumental in planning these works, and his death in 1938 coincided with its opening. This Bagnall, along with several sisters, formed part of the company's original locomotive roster.

Top: Though not part of Paraguay's main line system, the quebacho railways of the Paraguayan Chaco are little less fascinating. Here is No. 1, an 0-4-0 well tank named *Laurita* and built by Arthur Koppel of Berlin. The veteran carries a plate proclaiming that she was *la primera locomotora del Chaco Paraguayo* (the first locomotive on the Paraguayan Chaco).

Above: The cab-side name and number plate of the Ferrocarril Presidente Carlos Antonio Lopez's No. 152 *Ascunción*, built at the Yorkshire Engine Company's Meadowhall Works in Sheffield in 1953. This engine and her sister, *Encarnación*, were of distinctly LMS appearance.

PARAGUAY'S main line railway runs for 232 miles (371km) from the capital city of Ascunción to Encarnación, on the border with Argentina, and provided through services to Buenos Aires. Until the River Parana marking the border was bridged, a train ferry linked the two sides, wagons and carriages being lowered by a gentle inclined plane to the dock. Today, the final section to the Argentinean border is out of use. Little else has changed since British engineers converted the line from its original 5ft 6in gauge (1676mm) to standard gauge (1435mm) in 1910. A batch of Edwardian Moguls was exported from the North British Works in Glasgow, and some of these engines still remain in service.

The line has been allowed to run down for decades, and has reached an appalling state of disrepair; an average journey over the 232 miles could take 18 hours – an average speed of 13mph (21km/h). In 1953, the railway, known as the Ferrocarril Presidente Carlos Antonio Lopez, received two further Moguls from the Yorkshire Engineering Company's Meadowhall works in Sheffield. These engines, reminiscent of London Midland & Scottish Railway designs, were an updated version of the North British 1910 examples.

The works that maintain the railway are located in Sapucai, a tiny village some 50 miles (80km) from Ascunción. The erecting shop resembles that of a British locomotive builder from the nineteenth century. There is no electricity and the complete works – every drill and lathe – is worked by steam, provided by three stationary boilers standing in the overgrown works yard. Pride of place is a huge steam-hammer from Thwaites Brothers' Ironworks at Bradford in Yorkshire. At lunch-time the works' hooter resounds over the sleepy village, vividly recalling a Lancashire mill town at the turn of the century. The railway was under British ownership until 1961, and the works have a colonial atmosphere with a level of antiquity to match: ancient typewriters, Victorian desks and dusty files invoking a period long past.

The station at Ascunción is still well worth a visit, whether or not the trains are running. Built in Gothic style, its train shed resembles a modest-sized cathedral nave. On the platform is a 2-2-2 tank engine, reputedly Paraguay's first locomotive.

Right: North British-built Edwardian Mogul No. 103 rattles an Ascunción-bound freight out of San Salvador. Note the termite mound in the lower right-hand of the picture, which was taken on 22 January 1979.
Below: Hawthorn Leslie built the Ferrocarril Presidente Carlos Antonio Lopez's No. 5 – a delightful 2-6-2 tank of 1913. It is seen at Encarnación shunting of rake of wagons, which have just arrived from Argentina by paddle steamer across the mighty Parana River.

CLASSIC WORLD 10-WHEELERS

THE ten-wheeler, or 4-6-0, came to prevalence in America as the natural successor to the 4-4-0 once trains became more heavily loaded. By the 1890s, versions with small driving wheels for slower, heavy slogging as well as large-drivered examples with wheels of over 6ft (183mm) diameter were widely established in everyday service. However, the 4-6-0 was not as popular in the US as it was in Britain because of the inherent narrow firebox. For this reason, the US preferred the Pacific and Hudson types.

The first decade of the twentieth century saw 4-6-0s well-established in many parts of the world as a principal express passenger locomotive: Africa, Russia, the Indian subcontinent, Latin America and of course Europe, where such classic types as the Prussian P8s evolved.

In Britain, the 4-6-0 became the principal form of locomotive for express passenger work, but in contrast relatively few ever existed in Russia, China or Japan. In Europe, Germany and France were prolific users, while Italy was not, gravitating instead to the 2-6-2. The famous BESA standards set down in 1903 for the Indian subcontinent included a 4-6-0 express mail engine, the last derivations of were in use until the early 1980s.

Argentina, Chile and Brazil were all recipients of a broad variety of 4-6-0s, while Paraguay and Uruguay preferred Moguls, although in recent years Paraguay did receive some 4-6-0s second-hand from Argentina. In many parts of the world, 4-6-0s were eventually ousted by Pacifics on the top duties, while in other areas where trains were slower, the mixed-traffic Mikado with its potential for a wider firebox was preferred. By the late 1960s the 4-6-0 seldom appeared on steam rosters around the world. Today, it is absent from the closing ranks of world steam, with the exception of metre gauge examples in Pakistan and a couple of engines in Paraguay.

Above: Indian Railways have always held a fascination with their ability to make do and mend. The image of colourful locomotives, steam leaking from every gland, baking in the heat, is epitomized in this image of a classic BESA class 4-6-0.
Opposite: This thoroughbred Class 12A British 4-6-0 originally worked on the British-owned 5ft 6in (1676mm) gauge Buenos Aires & Great Southern Railway. Built by Beyer Peacock in 1906, the locomotive was originally a two-cylinder compound, and after withdrawal was purchased by the naval authorities for the base at Bahia Blanca where it was photographed in 1979.

EVERY male Moslem is required to visit Mohammed's birthplace in Mecca at least once in his life time. During the nineteenth century the journey was hazardous in the extreme. The Arabs were reluctantly under Ottoman rule and bands of vulnerable Turkish pilgrims were sometimes murdered as they journeyed through the desert. Eventually the Sultan of Turkey authorized the building of a railway between Damascus and Mecca to carry pilgrims in safety, though the railway had strong military and economic objectives. Construction of the line, built to the peculiar Levantine gauge of 3ft 5⅜in (1057mm), began to the south of Damascus in 1900, and after eight laborious years Medina, 820 miles (1,312km) from Damascus, was reached. Named the Hedjaz Railway, the line takes its name from the area alongside the Red Sea in Arabia where the holy city lies.

Trouble dogged every mile: marauding Arabs attacked the workers, the heat was intolerable and violent sand-storms frequently caused work to be stopped. The Arabs, frantic that their holy city would be defiled, refused to allow the railway past Medina. In wild fervour they invaded the railway construction camp and massacred the work force. The line was destined to go no further and pilgrims had to continue on foot over the remaining 230 miles (368km) to Mecca.

The railway carried pilgrims for only seven seasons before the outbreak of World War I. The Turks allied with Germany, and Arab nationalists, supported by the British under Col T.E. Lawrence, partly succeeded in driving them from the Hedjaz. To prevent enemy reinforcements from getting through, Lawrence blew up large sections of the line. So great was the damage that trains were forced to terminate at Ma'an in southern Jordan and, despite various attempts to reopen it, the southern section remains abandoned today.

Opposite: A Royal Jordanian Railway oil-burning Mikado heads a rake of phosphate wagons along the Hedjaz Railway.
Above: One of the two engines on a train which Lawrence of Arabia blew up south of Mudowwara, near the village of Haret Ammar, on 19 September 1917. According to Lawrence, this was the first engine of a double-headed train – the other locomotive being destroyed in the explosion under it. The engine seen here is 2-8-0 No. 110, built by Hartmann of Chemnitz in 1911 as their works' number 3545.

Above: An abandoned train on the Hedjaz Railway in Saudi Arabia at
Hadiyah Siding, which is set at right angles to the main line. The engine is
0-6-0 tank No. 17 built in Germany by Krauss in 1904 as their works'
number 5238.
Opposite: Royal Jordanian Railway No. 51, a Jung-built Mikado of 1955,
on a Qatrana to Amman passenger train comprised of original coaching
stock, as supplied new to the Hedjaz prior to World War I.

LES BELLES MACHINES *French Pacific locomotives*

The Paris, Lyons & Marseilles (PLM) Class 231 and sub-types were built between 1909 and 1932. Here we see a 231K, rebuilt from a 231C, leaving Calais docks for Paris at the head of the 'Fleche d'Or'. The magic of such continental journeys is now but a fond memory. Today the excitement centres around the Channel Tunnel and Eurostar.

THE French Pacifics possessed such power and majesty that seeing them in action was an unforgettable experience. They were known to French enginemen as 'les belles machines'. French Pacific tradition is rich in diversity and innovation, ever since Europe's first Pacifics were introduced by the Paris & Orléans in 1907. By 1910, 225 Pacifics were at work in France, and eventually the figure rose to 1,400, with over 1,000 left in 1950, despite considerable advances in electrification.

Locomotive history was made by André Chapelon of the Paris & Orléans when he revolutionized the design of many Pacifics by enlarging the internal steam circuits, redesigning the valves and boiler, introducing high degree superheat and revolutionizing the chimney blastpipe. ACFI feed-water heaters were also incorporated, and engines which had generated 2,000hp were transformed to develop 3,000hp. Chapelon's work spread far beyond France to exert a profound influence on steam locomotive design world-wide despite impending modernization and other modes of traction. The exploits of his redesigned Pacifics are legendary, such as working the 536-mile (858km) section between Paris and Marseilles at an average speed of 60mph (96km/h) with 400-ton expresses.

The four-cylinder compound 231Ks survived on the former Nord main line until 1969; amongst their rosters, they worked the English boat trains between Paris and Calais, such as the 'Golden Arrow', carrying the arrow on their smokebox door until their replacement by larger steam locomotives and diesels.

A brace of SNCF 231D class Pacifics form the centrepiece for this multi-modal transport scene at Dieppe harbour. The period 1950s atmosphere evokes the days when these elegant Pacifics worked the boat trains between Dieppe, Rouen and Paris.

AMERICAN SUPERPOWER

New Haven Railroad Class 1-5 4-6-4. These locomotives were the first streamlined 4-6-4s to be produced in the US in 1937. Normally, 1-5s were used for the crack expresses between New York and Boston.

AMERICAN steam 'Superpower' relates to four principal forms of locomotive: the freight-hauling Berkshire 2-8-4 and its extension to the Texas 2-10-4; the mixed-traffic Northern 4-8-4; and the passenger-hauling Hudson 4-6-4.

The term 'superpower' was coined by the locomotive builder Lima of Ohio, and it applied only to conventional engines; it did not embrace articulateds such as Mallets. Lima introduced the first Berkshire and Texas types in the mid-1920s to meet the need for faster and more powerful locomotives in the railways' struggle to hold their own against road competition, as well as cope with heavier coaching stock. Lima also intended its superpower to compete with Alco's huge three-cylinder types.

Lima introduced the first Berkshire with their A1, which was a super Mikado and the first engine of the superpower series. The first 2-10-4 locomotive went to the Texas & Pacific Railway, from which the name Texas for the type is derived.

The Northern 4-8-4 was a natural extension of the Mountain type (4-8-2) with extra boiler and firebox capacity. The first was built for the Northern & Pacific in 1927. Over the decades that followed, the Northern assumed some very powerful proportions and achieved a tractive effort of 85,000lb (38,555kg) on examples fitted with a booster.

The passenger-hauling Hudson was a super Pacific, and its huge firebox capacity provided for sustained high speeds and power output. However, less than 500 were built because of encroaching dieselization.

With these giants, the limits of the reciprocating steam locomotive was arguably reached. The rigid-framed Duplex divided drive was a late attempt to go a stage further, but it had little time to prove itself as diesels were rapidly becoming the favoured solution. The Duplex had disappeared by 1953, and by 1958 the superpower types had also been withdrawn. Ironically, all of these goliaths were outlived by some classic 4-4-0s of 1887, which survived in branch line service until 1961 – the very end of steam.

Southern Pacific GS-4 4-8-4 Confederation No. 4449 at Benson, Arizona, on 14 June 1984.

SCRAPYARDS

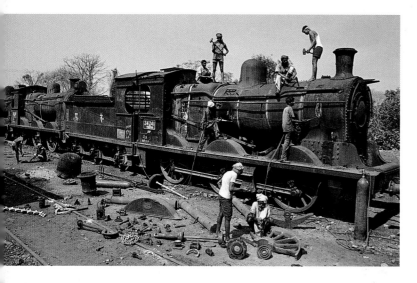

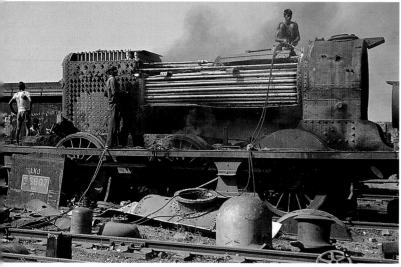

WHEN a locomotive comes to the end of its existence, its breaking-up releases varying grades of metal which are immediately recyclable. It was frequently said that many British engines which were broken up in Sheffield provided the raw material for the manufacture of prosaic razor blades.

Engines were scrapped in a wide variety of locations. Traditionally this had taken place at the railway company's locomotive works. Sometimes engines have been cut up at running sheds, often by outside contractors who take all the material away with them. Similarly, graveyards can be handed over to contractors who turn a tranquil weed-strewn place with its timeless atmosphere into a busy sea of activity with bustling men and cranes, where the wrench of tearing metal is accompanied by the bitter stench of acetylene gas.

Condemned engines were a familiar sight being towed to breakers' yards, one of the most famous of which was Dai Woodham's yard at Barry in South Wales. At its peak this huge mausoleum contained some 200 engines, which had been dragged there from many parts of Britain. At one time, railway works would conscientiously remove various good parts for reuse. Today, engines are often cut up piecemeal where they lie, as the need to remove spare parts for cannibalization has all but disappeared.

Sixty years ago nameplates and worksplates would often be thrown in with the scrap metal, railway administrations and demolition groups never dreaming that one day such items would be worth many thousands of pounds for their historic and aesthetic value.

Left above: A typically British inside-cylinder 0-6-0 and 'maid of all work' being broken up at the former East Indian Railway's works at Jamalpur.
Left centre: Another British-built inside-cylinder 0-6-0, withdrawn from Lucknow shed in 1976, is broken up at Sultanpur scrapyard.
Left: Cohen's scrapyard at Cransley near Kettering was one of the leading locomotive breaker's yards during the decline of steam in the 1960s. Here a brace of Stanier Black 5 4-6-0s are about to vanish under the torch during the last few years of steam operation.
Opposite: Pieces of locomotive anatomy lie abandoned in a Sudanese scrapyard.

SCRAPYARDS

Cutting up the one-time work horses of the British Raj at Shakur Basti on the outskirts of New Delhi in 1976. The next engine to be broken up looms in the background in the form of SGC class inside-cylinder 0-6-0 No. 36644, which was built by the Vulcan Foundry, Lancashire in 1912 for the Eastern Punjab Railway.

The remains of a China Railway's JF class 2-8-2 at Manzhouli in the north-eastern corner of China, close to the Russian border. The missing boiler has possibly been sold to an outside concern, the heating of all premises in this part of China during winter being of prime importance where temperatures fall to as low as −35°C.

PENSIONED OFF *From main line to industry*

MOST of the world's oldest locomotives have survived by being pensioned off from main line into industrial service in collieries and mineral workings. The practice of pensioning off locomotives does not normally cross national boundaries; relatively few railways have sold locomotives to foreign networks. There have been situations when this could – and probably should – have occurred, not least when leading Western countries dispensed with thousands of locomotives over a few years in their haste to be rid of steam. Some locomotives went to the breaker's yard when less than ten years old.

Engines that have been pensioned off internationally include a former New York Elevated Railway 0-4-4 tank that went to a Cuban sugar mill; the Soviet Railways FD class 2-10-2s, which were sent to China and regauged from the Russian 5ft (1524mm) gauge to China's 4ft 8½in (1435mm) standard gauge at Changchun Locomotive

Works; and some lovely Kerr Stuart 4-6-0s from Argentina's Urquiza Railway that went to Paraguay.

It is surprising that there have never been any internationally accepted standard types for services around the world. The closest to this ideal were the engines of the two world wars, which, surplus to military requirements, were dispersed hither and thither as aid or as reparations to aggrieved lands. Widespread post-war dispersals include the German Feldbahn and Kriegslokomotiv, along with the United States Army Transportation Corps 2-8-0s and 0-6-0 tanks, and the metre gauge McArthurs, all of which were widely scattered after cessation of hostilities.

Some remarkable transfers have occurred, like the ex-Indian Railways XB express passenger Pacific that ended up in an cement factory. India has some of the finest examples of historic engines in industrial service,

particularly in the sugar mills, where centenarians that began life on the private companies of British India in the nineteenth century remain hard at work, and two of these engines are 125 years old.

In Latin America some interesting main liners from the old Brazilian companies, like the Sorocabana and the Leopoldina, lingered on for many years in sugar plantation service in Campos State, while the world's last Texas type 2-10-4s, which transferred to Brazil's coal-carrying Dona Teresa Cristina Railway were from the former Central of Brazil.

One of the most wonderful engines pensioned off in world history was the beautiful Beyer Peacock two-cylinder compound 4-6-0 of the former Buenos Aires & Great Southern Railway (BAGS); built at Beyer Peacock's Gorton works in Manchester in 1906, it outlived its sisters by being transferred to shunt a high-security naval base.

Opposite: Late afternoon sunshine illuminates former Indian Railways HS class 2-8-0 No. 26128, built by Robert Stephenson at Darlington in 1914 for the Bengal Nagpur Railway, at Manikpur Mine on the Madhya Pradesh Electricity Board System based on Korba, in February 1989.
Above: A former South African Railway H2 class 4-8-2 tank shunts the exchange siding at Kromklip on the Tavistok Colliery network in May 1973. These engines were formerly 4-10-2s built in Glasgow for the Natal Government Railway.

PENSIONED OFF

Above: Kitson of Leeds built this delightful 2ft 6in (762mm) gauge 0-6-2 in 1900 for India's North Western Railway. Pensioned off into sugar plantation service, it was caught here far out on the plantations of the Saraya Sugar Mill in June 1977.

Opposite: One of the most famous locomotive types in world history was Major Marsh's United States Army Transportation Corps S160s, which were built to the British loading gauge for military operations during World War II. In common with most war engines, they were surplus to requirements, and the S160s spread to many parts of the world. China took a batch classifying them KD6, and here one is seen active on the Fushun mining complex, which includes the largest open-cast coal mine in the world. The Chinese have radically altered the appearance of these engines by adding a taller chimney, but in most other respects the engines are unchanged. Odd examples of this classic type remain in industrial service in China. This engine, belonging to the Fushun Mining Administration, was built by Lima of Ohio as their No. 8207 in May 1943. The picture was taken in −15°C on 5 January 1984.

SANKONG BRIDGE
The greatest train watching place in the world

SANKONG Bridge is a modest three-arched structure in the suburbs of Harbin, an important railway junction and the beautiful capital of Heilongjiang Province in north-eastern China. One peep over the parapet rolls the clock back 50 years, for the structure overlooks the vast marshalling yards, in which the endless streams of freights heading north and south are marshalled.

Harbin is popularly known as 'China's coldest city'. With daytime winter temperatures as low as –30°C, the biting Manchurian wind blows across the yard in vicious stinging blasts. In these conditions departing trains are unforgettable. The combination of steam spraying from the cylinder drain cocks, heavy-throated exhaust beats and musical chime whistles provide an audio-visual drama of the steam age without compare today. As giants pass beneath the bridge, with their exhausts occasionally in unison, but ususally in rhythmic polyphony, they enveloped the road in a steamy fog, bringing all traffic to a halt. Should a shunting or a trip movement happen to occur at the same time, it could be over a minute before activity can resume on the road.

On busy days a steam locomotive passes underneath the bridge every three minutes. Until the mid-1980s, modest JF Mikados, hump shunting 2,500 tonnes, would be seen slipping and occasionally stalling as they passed below the bridge with tortured exhaust beats.

The humping operations were fascinating. One could watch wagons of many different tyoes, bearing every conceivable type of merchandise, rolled in groups, first through king points, then queen points, before crossing primary and secondary retarders – dramas set against the amplified voice of the yard controller as he struggled to direct operations.

The magic of Sankong Bridge is elegantly summed up in this picture depicting a brace of China Railway's QJ 2-10-2s accelerating a 3,000-ton train southwards down the main line through Manchuria. The engines are allocated to Harbin depot and work as far south as Wujiatze. The wagons visible to the left and right form part of the hump shunting movements, and the wagons roll by gravity through King, Queen and Jack points.

PHANTOM ENGINES *From locomotive to stationary boiler*

Above: A raging sunset over the domed houses of the railway workers adds an eerie dimension to the stationary boiler in the shed yard at Sennar Junction on Sudan Railways. Sizzling and gently pulsating, the sense of unreality is heightened by the man silhouetted on the footplate. The boiler was taken from a locomotive built by North British of Glasgow in 1927.

Opposite: One of the world's rarest and most beautiful locomotives ended its days as this partially stripped hulk of Uruguay Railway's No.39, which languished next to the oil dock at Bella Vista depot in Montevideo, Uruguay. It was the world's last surviving 4-4-4 tank, a particularly harmonious form of now extinct locomotive, one of a batch built by the Vulcan Foundry, Lancashire in 1913 for working suburban trains around Montevideo. When this picture was taken on 10 February 1979 three sisters were lying condemned nearby. These were broken up soon afterwards, leaving this ghostly remnant as the sole survivor of its dynasty.

FROM the early days of railway history, a small number of locomotives on the point of retirement have been chosen for an extra lease of life as stationary boilers to produce hot water, drive machinery or to raise steam for heating. They took many forms: sometimes the engines were complete, but usually the wheels and motion would be removed, or possibly only the boiler would be used. Whatever the permutation, it was invariably placed in some shadowy corner of the depot or works, or down a remote weed-strewn siding. These ghosts of a bygone age would hiss and gurgle eerily in the gloom, and their weird shapes were guaranteed to terrify any small boy who might have stolen his way into the depot.

The most remarkable stationary boiler in world history was *Lion*, which worked on the Liverpool & Manchester Railway – the world's first all steam-operated passenger-carrying line – during the late 1830s. Withdrawn during the 1840s, *Lion* was used as a stationary boiler for pumping out Liverpool Docks. Some 85 years later, in 1935, the engine was 'discovered' a few weeks before it was due to be broken up for scrap. This veteran was saved and restored to working order and is now one of the world's most important preserved locomotives – there is almost none to match it in years.

Phantom engines

The story of *Lion* typifies the magic of the stationary boiler. Another remarkable survival was a Cambrian Railways 0-6-0 that languished outside Oswestry works on boiler duties, the last surviving example of its railway. A trip was organized from my school specially to the town on the Welsh Marches to see it, only to find that it had been broken up a few weeks previously. Little less exciting was the former London & North Western 'Cauliflower', a humble 0-6-0 goods locomotive, which stood for many years at the side of Saltley shed in Birmingham.

Today, stationary boilers remain in lands where steam power has disappeared. They are particularly prevalent in Russia and eastern Europe, where the harsh winters require an abundant supply of steam for heating both passenger stock and depots. Some boilers serve to maintain a supply of dry sand; this is required not only to help improve the grip on damp rails, but on oil-burning steam engines to throw into the firebox at periodic intervals to help to prevent furring of the boiler tubes by oil deposits.

Some locomotives have been sold off from railway service into separate industries and are waiting to be discovered. The history and purpose of stationary boilers is a fascinating aspect of the steam age and one that remains almost completely unresearched and undocumented.

Below: The boilers of many Ghana Railway's locomotives have been sold to sawmills to generate steam to power saws. This example, which came from the Vulcan Foundry, Lancashire in 1938, is at the A.E. Saoud Mill in Kumasi.

Opposite: A former South Eastern & Chatham Railway Stirling O class 0-6-0 relegated to stationary boiler service at Ramsgate for carriage heating. Ramsgate breakdown crane is in the background. The Os were a class of 20 0-6-0 goods engines, designed by Stirling and built by Sharp Stewart & Co., Glasgow, at a price of £2,050 each in 1878–9.

This fascinating hybrid operated at Springbok Colliery in the Transvaal. It was originally one of a batch of standard 4-8-2 industrial tanks exported from the North British works in Glasgow between 1937 and 1955. Many of these engines were later converted into tender engines by removal of the side tanks and the addition of improvised locally made four-wheel tenders. Loss of adhesion caused through removal of the side tanks was compensated for by false spashers containing some five tons of waste steel and concrete. Note that the engine's bunker is retained for carrying coal, the improvised tender being for water only. These hybrids were created both to prevent the dripping of water from the tanks on to the wheels and track, and to provide better adhesion, which was sometimes insufficient.

A typical colliery yard scene at Desford in the Leicestershire coalfields with the ubiquitous 0-6-0 saddle tank. Note the pit props in the immediate foreground.

OVER the first twenty years of the steam locomotive's existence, it worked solely in an industrial environment. It was not until 1825 that it emerged on to a 'main line' when the Stockton & Darlington Railway was opened. It is almost certain that when the world's last steam locomotive finally drops its fire it will be an industrial, steam having long finished on the world's main lines.

The industrial locomotive has served a wonderful diversity of locations, such as collieries, iron and steel works, quarries, plantations of sugar, rubber, and palm oil, docks, shipyards and forestry systems, along with a whole plethora of manufacturing industries.

Industrial railways are a fascinating and relatively under-documented subject. During the 'Railway Age', the attraction of the main and branch line systems was so great and diverse that the humble engines, largely hidden away trundling around a few miles of track within an industrial complex, were largely overlooked. Of course, once steam disappeared from the main line the industrial engine came into its own, although by then many of the more interesting examples had also disappeared.

Industrial steam locomotives fall into two distinct groups, each of which embrace a vast tapestry of designs and gauges. Firstly, there are engines built specifically for

WHEELS OF INDUSTRY

Below: A remarkable railway in northern Sumatra, built to convey stones from a river bed for use as ballast on the main lines of the Indonesian State railway. The engine is an 0-6-0 well tank from the German builder Orenstein & Koppel in 1920.

Right: This scene on the palm oil plantations of northern Sumatra shows an 0-4-4-0 Mallet heading a train of freshly harvested palm fruit on its way to the factory at Bah Djambi palm oil estate near Siantar. This and the picture below illustrate that by no means all of Indonesia's narrow gauge lines were built for sugar cane.

Opposite: Some of the world's largest deposits of iron ore lie in the jungles of Bihar – an estimated 2,500 million tons, believed to be 60 per cent iron in content. Under British rule a railway was built to exploit the deposits and these 0-4-2 tanks were exported from Andrew Barclay's works in Kilmarnock to work it. Here one is seen with the Indian Iron & Steel Corporation name emblazoned on its tank sides.

industrial service, and secondly, former main line engines pensioned off and sold to industrial concerns for a further lease of active life – these are portrayed separately on pages 226–9.

The traditional industrial engine is a tank of relatively modest proportions, this type being ideal for shunting and moving materials around confined areas. It is cheap to run, easily serviceable and manoeuvrable, and as fuel and water are carried on the main frame has good adhesion for moving heavy loads. The Fireless was an option for those industries with a ready supply of high pressure steam or a ban on sparks and cinders.

Though much less prevalent, tender engines were also used, especially on systems where longer running was involved, such as forestry railways or collieries which were distant from the main line railway. Although these tender engines were usually smaller than their main line counterparts, interesting exceptions have occurred, especially in China. Here the standard SY class industrial 2-8-2, of which upwards of 2,000 have been built, is a fully fledged light Mikado of the size and proportions used on the main lines of the US during the first two decades of the twentieth century. In many countries, engines the size of the SY would be rated as mixed-traffic main line power.

GERMAN PACIFICS *Mainstay of expresses*

Above: Deutsche Reichsbahn rebuilt Class 01.5 Pacific No 01.0534 heads a
Saalfeld-bound passenger train near Orlamunde in March 1981.
Opposite: Deutsche Reichsbahn Class 01 and its sister 02 express locomotives
were built from the mid-1920s. Eventually all were rebuilt to 01 configuration.
A Class 01 hauls an express through the German industrial heartland.

THE German Pacifics were a magnificent family of engines and the mainstay of Germany's steam expresses for some 40 years. The merger of Germany's railways in 1920 led to the introduction of a set of standard designs, amongst which were the famous O1 Pacifics, numbering 241 examples. Following World War II and the division of Germany, 171 passed to the western Deutsche Bundesbahn and 70 to the eastern Deutsche Reichsbahn.

During the speeding-up of Germany's express trains in the 1930s, civil engineers were concerned that hammer-blows from the two-cylinder O1s would damage the track, if allowed to run at speeds above their 81mph (130km/h) limit. Accordingly, in 1939 a three-cylinder streamlined version, classified O1.10 was built; 54 more followed by the end of 1940. Some O1s were later rebuilt with larger boilers; though an improvement, the modified engines were not nearly as handsome, although the East German ones were imposing with boxpok driving wheels, Giesl chimneys and modernistic smoke deflectors. The O1.10s lost their streamline casing by the early 1950s and during the 1960s they were also reboilered. The O1s were augmented by the O3 Pacifics, a lighter version of the O1.

The last high-speed expresses in Europe were operated between Berlin to Dresden until the late 1970s by 50-year-old Deutsche Reichsbahn O1s hand-fired on locally mined coal. They worked trains of up to 500 tons in weight on timings faster than a mile a minute (96km/h) with top speeds of 90mph (144km/h). This was the world's last great Pacific action.

BIRTHPLACE OF A LOCOMOTIVE *Datong, China*

THE magnificent spectacle of huge steam locomotives being built ended in Datong, the industrial town of Shanxi Province in north-western China close to the Inner Mongolian border. During the early 1980s the equivalent of one locomotive a day was emerging – a fascinating contrast to all other nations of the world which were phasing out steam as fast as they could. Small wonder that television crews descended on Datong to record the end of an age.

The activities at Datong were unforgettable. In the boiler shop, 20 boilers could be seen in varying stages of construction, inner and outer fireboxes contrasting with boiler shells, all illuminated and silhouetted in ghostly patterns by the welder's blinding flashes and set to a deafening cacophony of heavy drilling. It seemed very familiar to anyne who had known such establishments at places like Crewe, Derby, Doncaster or Swindon. Except

that at Datong the pace was unstoppable, and in a few hours a naked frame standing over the pits would be transformed into a fully fledged locomotive ready to be lifted on to its wheels in the erecting shop by overhead cranes driven by teenaged girls.

The giants would then be hauled into the steam testing sheds to receive their first breath of animation. Here they would stand hissing and gurgling in the gloom, decked in their workshop orange undercoats, before being taken on to the test track to be run up to high speeds prior to being returned to the works for full painting and ultimate dispatch on to the network.

Datong concentrated on JS 2-8-2s and QJ 2-10-2s and built 4,100 engines over about 25 years – over half the total produced by Crewe in 100 years. Datong had an 8,600-strong work force, 95 per cent of whom lived within the complex.

The magic that was Crewe Works in the early 1930s, as a Stanier Princess Royal Pacific No. 6207 *Princess Arthur of Connaught* enters the final stages of assembly in the erecting shop. These beautiful engines were Stanier's first Pacifics for the LMS and totalled 12 engines. On its test run, sister engine No. 6201 *Princess Elizabeth* covered the 401 miles from Glasgow to London Euston in 5$^1/_2$ hours – a start to stop average speed of over 70mph (96km/h).

Above: The erecting shop at Datong Works in China in the mid-1980s, when both QJ class 2-10-2s and JS class 2-8-2s were in production. At this time Datong was turning out an average of one locomotive a day. Here, a newly assembled QJ has just been lifted on to its wheels and will soon be ready to go to the steam testing shed.

Left: Datong Works, China, in January 1984, when a batch of JS Mikados was being built. The traditional American practice of bolting together cylinders and smokebox saddle are clearly visible in the foreground, as the unit for JS class No. 6604 waits to be craned into position. One could enter the erecting shop first thing in the morning to find a naked frame over the pits, but during the course of the day that frame would evolve into a fully fledged locomotive.

MASTODONS *America's heavy-duty freight power*

Argentine Railway's 11C class three-cylinder 4-8-0 No. 4222 heads an Olavarria to Loma Negra cement working in September 1978. She was built by Armstrong Whitworth of Newcastle-upon-Tyne in 1923. Seventy-five of these powerful locomotives were built for the 5ft 6in (1676mm) gauge Buenos Aires & Great Southern Railway during the 1920s – the last 20 being delivered from Beyer Peacock in 1927.

THE 4-8-0 wheel arrangement saw service in many parts of the world, but never actually ran in Britain, although it featured prolifically in that country's exports. The type was essentially a hill climber whose excellent flexibility and adhesion made it ideal for heavy hauling over light tracks with frequent curves. A flangeless pair of centre driving wheels offered additional flexibility. The type was built for over a century and is believed to have totalled some 5,000 locomotives.

Predictably, the first major application of the 4-8-0 was in the United States, where the type became established during the late nineteenth century. Also known as the 'Twelve-wheeler', the name 'Mastodon' is taken from an engine built by the Central Pacific Railway in 1882. The 4-8-0 represented America's heaviest freight power until the last few years of the nineteenth century.

Suitable operating conditions for 4-8-0s were encountered in most areas of the world. In Africa, it appeared prolifically in many forms throughout the continent. It was also used, though to a lesser extent, in Latin America; Brazil and Peru were users, as was Argentina where some latter-day designs were of this type, especially the superb Class 15 and Class 11C three-cylinder examples, both of which remained active into the 1980s. In all, some 400 were built for service in Latin America.

In Europe, some extremely impressive engines were eventually produced, notably in France and the Austro-Hungarian Empire, where the last examples were the celebrated Hungarian Class 11s. The 4-8-0 never made an appearance in Germany, although that country's builders exported examples to various parts of the world. The Prussian State Railways considered a 4-8-0 version of the P8 4-6-0s, but it was never built. The type has a particularly long history in Spain, where it first appeared in 1912, and remained on that country's active roster until steam was displaced. Turkey's terrain also favoured use of the 4-8-0 type and some magnificent German-built examples were exported there in the 1920s.

Today the 4-8-0 is all but extinct, having been generally replaced in the last years of steam development by the Mikado and Mountain types, which offered similar flexibility, but better boiler proportions, once the axle weights could be increased as railway structures and track were progressively strengthened.

Argentine Railway's 15B class 4-8-0 No. 1583, built by the Vulcan Foundry of Newton-le-Willows, Lancashire, in 1948, prepares to depart from Las Flores at the head of an Olavarria to Tolosa freight. These 4-8-0s were one of the types which brought the vast tonnage of wheat, fruit and beef from the Argentine pampas to the Atlantic coast for export across the world when Argentina was a leading world economy.

THE RELICS OF SENNAR JUNCTION

Above: Abandoned engines at Meadow Corner included 220 class Pacific No. 256 and an 0-6-0
tank from Hunslet of Leeds, No. 7. The picture was taken on 9 January 1983.
Opposite: Old Sennar Junction station board with a 220 class Pacific in the shed yard behind.

SUDAN'S railways were British-built, and Atbara, where
the main works are loacted, was one of Africa's most
industrialized towns. The country's vast railway system
extends from the Egyptian border in the north to Wau in
the south, and from the Red Sea town of Port Sudan in the
east to the western town of Nyala, near the border with
Chad. Atbara was such a prominent works in the British
empire that a Great Western Railway locomotive was
named after the place.

Sennar is the most important junction on the system,
connecting the principal north–south and east–west routes.
The depot's roster was comprised of British engines,
seven of the 220 class Pacifics introduced in 1927 and three
of the 310 class Mikados of 1952, the two classes sharing
a common boiler. Also present was a 2-6-4 tank
from Kitson of Leeds in 1931 with a delightful British
colonial appearance.

At the far end of the shed, several engines were dumped
in an area known as 'Meadow Corner', and here lay another
standard Sudanese design in the form of an 0-6-0 shunter,
one of a class of 30 introduced in 1927 by Hunslet of Leeds.
These engines continued to be delivered until as late as
1951, which is particularly interesting as Sudan was an early
recipient of diesel shunters in the 1930s. These 0-6-0s were
one of the last classic main line shunting tanks ever built.

The shed yard was dominated by one of the most
amazing stationary boilers. Seen against the triangular-
shaped dwellings of the railway compound, it made an
almost surreal sight and is depicted on page 232.

THE GROWTH OF THE MALLETS

A bright sunny morning at Pesantren sugar mill in Kediri finds Mallet No. 194 in the cane transfer yard. A classic Mallet, it is a four-cylinder compound 0-4-4-0 tank, built by Orenstein & Koppel in 1920. Java's Pesantren mill was one of the few places on earth where yellow-liveried engines could be found.

IN 1887, the Swiss engineer Anatole Mallet devised a 60cm (1ft 11⅝in) gauge semi-articulated compound 0-4-4-0 tank engine, in which the main frames were split into two units – the rear one rigid, carrying the high-pressure cylinders, and the leading one articulated and bearing the low-pressure cylinders. Whether compound or simple, tank or tender, Mallets proliferated for main line and industrial use throughout most of the world.

The growth of the Mallet, which like the Garratt was ideal for operating over lightly laid and sharply curved tracks, was phenomenal with over 5,000 examples being built. South Africa was an early user of Mallets, and by 1909 a 130-ton example had appeared on that country's 3ft 6in (1067mm) gauge railways. Three years earlier, 180-ton giant Mallets had begun appearing in America, so beginning that country's long affair with the type. As the Garratt colonized Africa, the Mallet colonized America with over 3,000 fully developed main line examples being built, eventually flowering into the biggest steam locomotives of all time – the Union Pacific 4-8-8-4 Big Boys, which weighed 550 tons in full working order.

In common with the Garratt, Mallets can still be found in service, interestingly in the form of small compounds taking the concept back to where it started over a century ago. The sugar fields of Java support a number of 0-4-4-0 Mallet tanks while Eritrea's revitalized railway has put the Mallet back into 'main line' service.

No. 204 was one of six giant metre gauge four-cylinder simple Mallets delivered by Baldwin to Brazil's Teresa Cristina Railway between 1941 and 1949. They were specifically for working the heavily graded and tightly curved line from Tubarao to Lauro Muller. In 1974 the track to Lauro Muller was washed away during violent storms and the cost of repairing the line was higher than the value of the dwindling reserves of coal. These unique Mallets were made redundant, and when this picture was taken, in December 1978, No. 204 – one of the last survivors – was relegated to tripping work around the Teresa Cristina system.

INDUSTRIAL WORKHORSES OF CHINA

A pair of begrimmed Chinese SY class industrial Mikados stand in front of the blast furnaces at Anshan Iron & Steel Works during a brief respite from their duties. During the 1980s, production from this vast complex was an unbelievable 13.85 million tons of iron and steel a year – the complex includes 10 blast furnaces, 3 steel mills and 20 rolling mills. Ninety per cent of the ore is mined locally and conveyed to the works by an electrified railway system.

China's iron and steel works at Anshan is one of the most exciting industrial complexes, with a truly fascinating range of locomotives ranging from vintage 'crocodile' overhead DC electrics to small 0-6-0 tanks. The steam roster includes some very rare industrial Praires, and here a PL2 class 2-6-2 is seen waiting to draw ladles of liquid iron from the blast furnaces.

INDUSTRIAL locomotives in China are found at a huge diversity of rail-connected concerns, and in mid-1998 there were thought to be upwards of 2,000 locomotives left in industrial service. While the SY class Mikado predominates at the vast majority of such locations, a few are worked by older types, such as the United States Army Transportation Corps 0-6-0 tanks and Major Marsh's S160 2-8-0s, albeit in ever-dwindling numbers.

Even older are some former main line Mikado classes, such as the JF, which has virtually vanished from the main lines. There is also the smaller Japanese-built JF6, which is descended from a standard American Locomotive Co. design originally supplied to Korea. JF6s worked on the Japanese-controlled South Manchurian Railway and Manchurian National Railways during the 1930s. The SY is descended from this type.

The PL2 class is unusual in being an industrial Prairie and is believed to be a rebuild of the JF6. The YJs are a similar class of industrial Prairies. One of the rarest industrials are the 0-4-0 Fireless engines at Benxi Steel Works. One of these is believed to have been built by Borsig of Berlin in 1916 and is probably the oldest locomotive left working in China.

On the 762mm (2ft 6in) gauge, a fine variety of provincial and forestry railways use a standard type of 28-ton 0-8-0, built in eastern Europe and China. The design of these engines was based on the Soviet PT4s. China also has a 40-ton version with bar-frames; these engines are similar to the well-known Polish narrow gauge PX48s.

THE MIKADOS *Maids of all work*

THE Mikado 2-8-2 was the most popular locomotive type built in America after 1900, with some 14,000 examples including those for export. Mikados constituted some 8 per cent of the 170,000 steam locomotives produced by the United States. The type name is taken from Gilbert and Sullivan's *Mikado*, which was popular in the US at the time that Baldwin exported some 2-8-2s to Japan in 1897.

The Mikado was primarily a freight type, although on secondary work where speeds were not of particular relevance, they formed an excellent mixed-traffic locomotive. US Mikados split into two basic categories: the heavy Mikados, which played a leading role in main line service and the light Mikados, which were introduced for secondary routes. In common with other leading types, some main line Mikados gravitated on to secondary lines as train weights and sizes grew progressively heavier. The type was not suited to high driving wheels, and 66in (168cm) was generally taken as the maximum for stability.

The Mikado was a great improvement on the 2-8-0s, which it often replaced, and its heyday in the land of its origin dated roughly from the beginning of the century until the early 1930s, with the more powerful examples being introduced after 1911.

As late as 1920, the average freight train speed in the United States was only around 20mph (32km/h), and as road competition began to threaten rail, bigger Mikados with large fireboxes boosted this to a sprightly 40mph (64km/h) on many routes, and with trains which were 50 per cent heavier. The larger Mikados had grate areas of over 70sq ft (6.5m^2) and were mechanically stoked. The Mikado was developed further during the 1920s when Lima introduced the 2-8-4 Berkshire, which had a two-axle swivelling truck to allow even more generous furnaces.

The Mikado, like the Pacific, appeared in most parts of the world, often in large numbers. Many of these were either US exports or derived from US practice, reflecting the influence that country had over locomotive around the world. In China, the type has assumed great importance, both through Japanese influence – which in turn was derived from the US – and subsequent building at home. The Chinese JS class continued to be built until the late 1980s and the SY class industrial, a modern equivalent of a US light Mikado of the early twentieth century, is still being built today.

Interestingly, Russia was one major land mass on which the Mikado was conspicuously absent.

Left: An SNCF 141R class Mikado. Following the ravages of World War II, France's 17,000 steam locomotives were reduced to 3,000 serviceable ones when the Germans evacuated. The French appealed to America for some simple robust mixed-traffic engines. The response was rapid, and a total of 1,340 141Rs were delivered by 1947.

Following pages: Cumbres & Toltec Railroad Class K36 2-8-2 No. 489 relettered in the style of the former 'Rio Grande' captured at Dalton on this 64-mile (102km) long railway straddling the States of New Mexico and Colorado, the territory of the old Denver & Rio Grande Railroad.

Opposite: The American railroad scene has always been a fascination for the sheer size of its locomotives and the vast distances covered. In this scene. which was played every night across the states between the two world wars, a 'Mike' leads its load of boxcars through the network of tracks on the outskirts of a city.

Right: This 3-foot (900mm) gauge Baldwin Mikado was built in 1927 and works on the 80-mile (128km) long Huancayo to Huancavelica Railway in Peru. This fascinating railway traverses narrow gorges, swirling river torrents, tunnels, bridges and abounds in steep grades.

First published in Great Britain in 1998
by Weidenfeld & Nicolson

This paperback edition first published in 1999 by
Seven Dials, Cassell & Company
The Orion Publishing Group
Wellington House, 125 Strand
London, WC2R 0BB

A CIP catalogue record for this book is available from the British Library
ISBN 1 84188 029 9

Designed by: Price Watkins
Edited by: Anthony J. Lambert
Printed and Bound in: Italy
Set in: Garamond ITC and Gill Alternative

Picture credits

All photographs are by Colin Garratt/Milepost 92^1/$_2$ unless otherwise stated. All paintings are by Terry Hadler.
Philip J. Ashworth: 215, 216.
A. E. Durrant: 22, 34, 36, 37, 43, 177.
G. Holme: 204.
Anthony J. Lambert: 45, 60, 65 (centre left), 74, 88 (left), 119, 142.
Richard Pelham: 217.
David C. Rodgers: 2–3, 7, 62–3, 94, 96–7, 139, 165, 188, 240, 254–5.
Mike Spencer: 89.
R. Tourret: 214.
Ron Ziel: 13, 29, 54, 106, 107, 125, 132, 146–7, 153, 154, 167, 178 (bottom), 180, 181, 182, 183, 206, 221.
Public Record Office: 99 (top right).

Colin Garratt exclusively uses Canon Eos cameras and lenses and Agfachrome RS professional film